FREE TO BE
MUHAMMAD
ALI

Robert Lipsyte

An Ursula Nordstrom Book

HARPER & ROW, PUBLISHERS
New York, Hagerstown, San Francisco, London

Library of Congress Cataloging in Publication Data
Lipsyte, Robert.
    Free to be Muhammad Ali.

    "An Ursula Nordstrom book."
    SUMMARY: A biography of a boxer who has come to be know as "The
Greatest."
        1. Ali, Muhammad, 1942–   —Juvenile literature.
2. Boxers (Sports)—United States—Biography—Juvenile
literature. [1. Ali, Muhammad, 1942–   2. Boxers
(Sports)] I. Title.
GV1132.A44L56 1978   796.8′3′0924 [B] [92]   77-25640
ISBN 0–06–023901–8
ISBN 0–06–023902–6 lib. bdg.

Contents

For Ursula Nordstrom,
A Champion in a class of her own

Ali and Me/
An Introduction

One afternoon in 1975, a Federal officer walked into Muhammad Ali's dressing room in the Fifth Street Gym in Miami Beach and handed him a subpoena in a lawsuit he eventually won. Ali, who was stretched out on a rubbing table, handed it to me.

"See how I take care of you, Bob?" he said. "When you're with me you always got something to write about."

What he said was absolutely true, and is the best way to describe our relationship. I began tagging along behind him taking notes in 1964, when he was a loud-mouthed contender named Cassius Clay and I was a young sportswriter for *The New York Times*.

He is far and away the most interesting character in that mythical kingdom I call SportsWorld, and his declaration after winning the championship—"I'm free to be who I want"—was the single most important statement of the so-called Athletic Revolution in which athletes began to liberate themselves from the phony roles and false values imposed upon them by owners and coaches and journalists and fans.

He was also a window on the 1960's and 1970's in America; his life touched and was touched by the civil rights movement, the anti-Vietnam War movement, the rise of the gold-plated age of sports, and the television takeover of entertainment and thought. A reporter could hardly ask for more.

People always ask me if I like him. The answer has always been Yes. He is courteous and helpful and fun to be with. People ask me if I think he is the greatest fighter of all time. He is certainly the greatest fighter of *my* time, and from the films I've seen of Jack Johnson and Jack Dempsey and Joe Louis I have to think Ali could have beaten them all. And people ask me what Ali is *really* like. To that question I answer: I don't really know. And I'm not sure that he really knows, either.

Muhammad Ali is a wise man and a fool, a person of principle and a greedy huckster, a generous, miserly, smart, silly, kind, cruel spirit of our times who has described himself both as "the king of all kings" and as "just another nigger trying to get bigger."

Somewhere in there is a little boy from Louisville, Kentucky, who started out, as I did and you did, just trying to be somebody special.

1

The Olympic Nigger

Cassius Marcellus Clay, Jr., the prettiest, The Fastest, THE GREATEST, burst upon the world in the summer of 1960, at the Olympic Games in Rome.

The world was fascinated.

He was big, handsome, and charming. He was an 18-year-old poet with a dazzling smile and fists like hammers. He was a motor-mouth who could back up every word—he said he would win the light-heavyweight boxing gold medal, and he did it with stunning ease.

When a Soviet journalist digging for controversy asked him about racial segregation in America, Cassius answered: "Tell your readers we got qualified people working on that, and I'm not worried about the outcome.

"To me, the U.S.A. is still the best country in the

world, including yours. It may be hard to get something to eat sometimes, but anyhow I ain't fighting alligators and living in a mud hut."

Years later he would regret that quote, and apologize for it and attribute it to ignorance, but as it flashed around the world that summer of 1960, Cassius Clay became a hero, a symbol of what was right about America.

Here was a young black man, the descendent of slaves, who seemed properly grateful for the advantages of democracy. He wasn't agitating to vote or sitting in at lunch counters. He was knocking down Communist boxers in the Olympic Games, those pretend World Wars, and he stood straight and proud when the star-spangled banner was waved to celebrate his victory.

He seemed like the perfect man-child for a curious time.

America was teetering on the brink of that tumultuous decade, the Sixties: Long-simmering racial unrest was about to boil into the streets, and the Cold War between America and the Communist countries was heating up; anti-American feeling was high among the developing nations of Asia and Africa and South America, and at home Richard M. Nixon and John F. Kennedy were slugging it out in the final rounds of their brutal Presidential campaign.

No wonder the newspapermen who would later attack Muhammad Ali found Cassius Clay so charming, delightful, innocent, in 1960. They would always hark back to the joyous and playful Clay of that Roman summer as if the "hateful" Ali were not a further development of the very same person.

They would scratch their heads, those white, middle-class, middle-aged journalists, and they would wonder how Cassius Clay "went wrong."

They liked to remember how Clay wore his Olympic gold medal even to bed, and they wrote and rewrote his mock-sorrowful explanation of why he finally took it off: "I wasn't sleeping too good. I had to sleep on my back because the medal would cut into me when I tried to sleep on my stomach."

But somehow they never wrote, at least not in 1960, that when Cassius returned to Louisville, Kentucky, after the Olympics, he still couldn't get served in the segregated restaurants of his hometown.

Even with that gold medal on his chest he couldn't eat with white folks.

He had proven himself the best boxer of his class in the world, but back home he was referred to as "that Olympic nigger."

From the top of the world to the bottom of the heap.

From champion back to "boy."

2

A Boy and a Bike

Cassius Clay was born on January 17, 1942.
"Ohhhhhhh, he was a *big* baby," says his mother,
Odessa. "So active. Into everything. Always running.
Jabbering away even before he could talk. He had a
knockout punch when he was six months old.

"See these front teeth of mine? We were lying in bed
and he hit me so hard they pushed apart, and then the
dentist had to pull 'em out."

His father, Cassius, Sr., recalls, "First words he said
were 'Gee Gee.' He was trying to tell us he was going
to win the Golden Gloves."

Cassius himself dates his interest in boxing to a
rainy day in 1954 when his brand-new red Schwinn
bicycle was stolen from a Louisville street corner. He
had left it outside while he gorged himself on free

popcorn at the annual Home Show. When he came out, the bike was gone.

He stopped a passerby. You seen a red Schwinn? The man shook his head and suggested he go down to the basement, to the Columbia Gym. There's a policeman down there named Joe Martin. He might be able to help.

Cassius raced downstairs and burst into the Columbia Gym. He caught his breath at the explosions of movement and sound.

A dozen youngsters, black and white, jumped and twisted and jerked around, bells rang, ropes *swish-slapped* against the squeaking floorboards, gloved fists slammed into a heavy leather bag with a meaty *thud,* against a speed punching bag that caromed off wood with a machine-gun *rackety-rackety-rack.*

In a ring set in the middle of the gym, a shadow-boxer threw punches faster than Cassius could follow them. Voices shouted "TIME!" and "Faster, stick and move, jab, jab, jab."

Cassius was spellbound, uncharacteristically silent and still. Only his nose twitched at the heady stench of sweat and rubbing alcohol and liniment. It was a few minutes before he remembered what had brought him here in the first place. He found Joe Martin.

"Somebody stole my bike, only got it two days ago, cost sixty dollars, when I find him I'm gonna whup him, I'm gonna . . ."

Joe Martin nodded patiently. Although he was not on duty at the moment, he filled out a report. He looked Cassius over. "Do you know how to box?"

"No, but I'd fight him and whup him and . . ."

"Why don't you come down here and start training," said Martin. "We've got boxing every night, Monday through Friday, from six to eight."

He gave Cassius an application blank. The twelve-year-old stuck it in a back pocket and edged out of the gym, glancing over his shoulder, unaware he had found his future.

3

Tomorrow's Champions

The red Schwinn bicycle was never recovered. And the application blank stayed in Cassius' back pocket and was eventually tossed, with the dirty pants, into the laundry basket. Cassius' first glimpse of his future was quickly smothered in the fury of his father's anger. Sixty dollars was no small matter to the Clays.

Cassius Marcellus Clay, Sr., earned a living as a sign painter. He had managed to buy his own home, but he could never get enough money together to have the sagging back porch repaired, or the erratic bathroom plumbing fixed.

An artist of some talent, he bitterly resented hauling his buckets and drop cloths all over town in the back of a ten-year-old car when he felt he should be getting rich and famous as a muralist and portrait painter.

A glib, handsome man, Cassius, Sr., felt demeaned

because his wife had to clean houses at four dollars a day to help make ends meet. He saw himself as the victim of an oppressive white society that unfairly judged him by the color of his skin rather than by his artistic gifts.

When young Cassius slunk back home, bikeless, he probably got a tongue-lashing from his father that began as a tirade against carelessness and escalated into a speech on racial injustice in America.

As he had on so many other occasions during Cassius, Jr.'s childhood, Cassius, Sr., may also have slammed out of the house. Perhaps he went to his favorite tavern, where he was appreciated as a flashy dancer, a crooner with a trace of Nat (King) Cole in his husky voice, and a smoothy with women.

After the theft, Cassius hung around the house, chastened and without wheels. That following Saturday he was watching a local television program called *Tomorrow's Champions*, an amateur boxing show. He noticed Joe Martin, the off-duty policeman he had met at the Columbia Gym, crouching in a corner with one of the young fighters, whispering advice and shouting encouragement.

Cassius jumped out of his chair.

"Bird!" he yelled to his mother. "You seen a piece of paper in my pants?"

Odessa Grady Clay, a gentle, pillowy woman called Bird by her sons (" 'Cause she's as sweet and pretty as a bird," they explain) nodded and smiled. She had removed the application blank from Cassius' pocket before washing the pants. She knew how careless he was with papers and money and even valuable possessions, like bicycles.

Cassius had little trouble talking his parents into signing the application. He was a highly energetic boy with a short attention span in school; free boxing lessons supervised by a policeman seemed like a positive alternative to running with gangs or loafing on street corners.

The next Monday evening, Cassius returned to the Columbia Gym. He brought his brother, ten-year-old Rudolph Arnet Clay. Cassius pulled on his first pair of boxing gloves and leaped into the ring with an older, more experienced boxer. He didn't last a round.

Dizzy, his mouth bruised, blood streaming from his nose, Cassius was hauled out between the ropes.

"At that moment I was thinking I'd be better off in the streets," he recalled much later, "but a slim welterweight came up and put his arms around my shoulders saying, 'You'll be all right. Just don't box these older fellows first. Box the fellows who are new like you. Get someone to teach you how to do it.' "

Cassius' first teacher was Joe Martin, then a thirty-six-year-old traffic patrolman. Lively, enthusiastic, Martin had passed up promotions on the police force to concentrate on his first love, boxing. He had built the gym into a thriving fight factory by hard work, a passion for the sport, and a selfless dedication to his boys.

As producer of the TV show *Tomorrow's Champions*, Martin had an edge on every other boxing manager in town—he could promise his fighters four dollars a bout and the instant celebrity of a television appearance.

Martin had, according to Cassius, the "complexion and connections to give me protection and direction." It was the same refrain he later used to describe the Louisville millionaires who sponsored his early professional career. Like Martin, the millionaires were white.

Nowadays Ali claims that Patrolman Martin was able to teach him very little about the techniques of boxing and that his immediate success as an amateur was based more on the raw dynamism of his flailing, windmill style than on any training he got at the Columbia Gym. From the start, Cassius was an aggressive competitor who never quit, who wore down most of his opponents—either physically or psychologically.

His real boxing teacher, he says, was Fred Stoner, a black trainer with a shabby little community-center gym in "Snake Town," the poorest of Louisville's black ghettoes.

This may or may not be true. The stories that Cassius Clay/Muhammad Ali has told about himself, and the stories that have been told about him—including those in such authorized works as his autobiographical book and film *The Greatest*—are very often too good to be true.

They are part of the "fakelore" that has grown up around a man whose life is so often displayed as a symbol. And Ali, who has heard so many versions of his life, may not always know himself what is authentic and what has been fictionalized.

Years ago, Cassius Clay gave a great deal of credit to Joe Martin. Nowadays, Muhammad Ali says he used to sneak out of Martin's gym to get secret lessons from Stoner.

And to complicate matters even further, Fred Stoner began working for Joe Martin in the 1970's, and both men tend to deny the story that Cassius was more of a Stoner fighter than a Martin fighter.

In any case, we can be sure of one thing: Three months after twelve-year-old Cassius Clay stumbled into the Columbia Gym to report a stolen bicycle, he appeared as a fighter on Martin's program, *Tomorrow's Champions.*

Young Cassius' preparation for that first fight was a sneak preview of the spectacular self-promotion that later hyped his multimillion-dollar title bouts. For a week he marched around Louisville, knocking on doors, buttonholing strangers, and interrupting conversations to exclaim: "I'm Cassius Clay, and I'm having a fight on television. I hope you'll watch me."

If the door wasn't slammed shut in his face, he would continue with the date, the hour, and the channel.

And, most important, the prediction that he would win.

"It's safe to say," said Joe Martin, "that Cassius believed in himself right from the beginning. If boxers were paid bonuses on their potential, like ballplayers are, I don't know if he would have received one.

"He was just ordinary and I doubt whether any

scout would have thought much of him in his first year. But after that time I realized it was almost impossible to discourage him. He was easily the hardest worker of any kid I ever taught, and I've taught hundreds in my time."

After a moment's reflection, Martin added, "Even then he was a little on the smart-alecky side, but he was a kid willing to make the sacrifices necessary to achieve something worthwhile in sports."

That very first fight on television was against one Ronny O'Keefe. It went three rounds, to a split decision.

Predictably, the winner was Cassius Clay.

4

The Road to Rome

If there had been any misgivings at all in the Clay household about Cassius punching and being punched, they evaporated in the flush of that first victory.

The elder Cassius now boasted in the taverns, "My son is going to be another Joe Louis. World, get ready for a heavyweight champion named Cassius Clay."

Odessa began pointing out to people that Cassius had "a big round head just like Joe Louis'."

A crude but crowd-pleasing slugger, Cassius soon became a regular on *Tomorrow's Champions*, and a neighborhood celebrity. Gang members respected him, teachers overlooked his unsatisfactory schoolwork and, perhaps most important, he gained recognition within his father's large and accomplished family of teachers, musicians, craftspeople, and business owners.

While Ali has angrily denied descriptions of his upbringing as "middle class," and countered them with stories of wearing secondhand clothing from Goodwill Industries and missing meals because there was no money in the house, there is no doubt that the Clays were never hopelessly poor. Cassius' parents were able to give him moral support, structure, and the belief that if he tried hard enough he would succeed.

They also gave him pride.

The first reporter to prospect deeply into Clay's background, Jack Olsen of *Sports Illustrated*, discovered that several members of the family traced themselves back to Henry Clay, the five-time Presidential aspirant known as "The Great Compromiser."

Well before Emancipation, so the family story goes, Cassius Marcellus Clay, a white kinsman of Henry Clay, freed his slaves, including a Negro son of Henry's who took his former master's name and passed it on.

Muhammad Ali bridles at such genealogy, although he does not categorically deny it. He claims that the family rarely talked about such matters, and if there is any "white blood . . . it came by rape and defilement."

Ali prefers to dwell on less remote ancestors, such as grandfather Herman Clay, who cleaned downtown Louisville cuspidors for twenty-five cents a week yet saved enough money to start his own ice-and-wood business.

16

Herman never forgot how badly whites had treated him, and he would not allow them into his home.

Conditioned by the experiences of his father and his grandfather, motivated by the success of his Uncle Everett, a university mathematician, and Aunt Coretta, who owned a restaurant, young Cassius channeled his energies toward a future goal—a boxing championship.

He rose at five A.M. to run in the park, and he raced alongside the bus the twenty-eight blocks to school, where he dozed through his classes to lunchtime, when he ran again.

In the afternoons and on weekends he earned pocket money mowing lawns and mopping floors at a Catholic school called Nazareth College, now known as Catherine Spalding College. The nuns still remember him shadowboxing at the glass bookcases in the library and proudly setting up his boxing trophies for display in the hallways.

In the early evenings, Cassius trained with Joe Martin at the Columbia Gym. Later at night he may—or may not—have also trained secretly with Fred Stoner.

Whether he did or not (or worked out with Stoner only occasionally), his skinny body filled out and became muscled. His natural energy and speed were transformed into lightning punches and dazzling footwork. His quick mind, never stimulated by standard education, was nourished through the study of boxing. He became a "student of the game," which is unusual among athletes who have great natural ability.

He haunted gyms to watch other fighters, pored

over pictures of past champions, and badgered trainers, managers, ex-boxers, for advice and shoptalk.

He developed a technique of leaning backward to avoid a punch rather than "slipping" it, the more orthodox maneuver in which a fighter moves his head to the side. When trainers warned him that he would someday get his head knocked off, he quietly reminded them that Jack Johnson, perhaps the greatest heavyweight of them all, had leaned backward and done just fine.

He was smart and strong. He had natural ability and the will to work hard. But most important, he had self-confidence.

He read in the newspaper one day that the famous trainer Angelo Dundee was in Louisville with his latest champion, the light heavyweight Willie Pastrano. He ran to their hotel and called them from the lobby.

"This is Cassius Clay, the next heavyweight champion talking," he said. "I'm gonna win the Olympics and be heavyweight champ. I'm in the lobby. Can I come up?"

Even now, Dundee shakes his head in wonderment when he tells the story. "Can you believe that? Can you believe he was fifteen years old at the time?"

Clay was invited up, and he spent the next several hours pumping Dundee and Pastrano about training methods, boxing lore, and trade secrets. Within a few years Pastrano would be his friend, Dundee would be his trainer, and all his predictions would be history.

But beneath the warm, positive stories of Cassius'

boyhood ran a darker current. His home life was not quite the jolly TV sitcom he now describes. His father was a mercurial personality with an occasional drinking problem. There were several violent incidents in his life. Cassius and Rudy, who seems always to have lived in his brother's shadow, favored the sweeter, more stable moods of their mother.

If his father's house was not always a snug harbor, then the world outside was truly filled with rebuff and sometimes danger. There were racial slights on the streets of Louisville, and no matter how many times he starred on *Tomorrow's Champions* there were restaurants, cheap, sleazy restaurants, that would not serve him because he wasn't white.

Perhaps the single most shocking racist incident during his youth was the murder of Emmett Till, a fourteen-year-old black youth from Chicago who was visiting relatives in Greenwood, Mississippi, in August 1955.

A rumor spread that Emmett had insulted a white woman. Three white men dragged him from his relatives' home and drowned him.

Despite witnesses and the FBI's carefully documented case, local all-white juries acquitted the three men of the murder and refused to indict them even for kidnapping.

Black newspapers and magazines covered the case extensively and Cassius, Sr., discussed it for weeks, dramatizing the crime in his flamboyant style and impressing on his sons the lesson of unequal justice.

Young Cassius, who was almost the same age as Emmett Till, was haunted by photographs of the dead boy's swollen, smashed face.

"I couldn't get Emmett out of my mind, until one evening I thought of a way to get back at white people for his death," wrote Ali in his autobiography, *The Greatest*. With his closest boyhood friend, Ronnie King, he broke into the shoeshine boys' shed at the West Side railroad station and stole two iron shoe rests. They planted them on the tracks and waited.

"When the big blue diesel came around the bend, it hit the shoe rests and pushed them nearly thirty feet before one of the wheels locked and sprang from the track. I remember the loud sound of ties ripping up. I broke out running, Ronnie behind me, and then I looked back. I'll never forget the eyes of the man in the poster staring at us: UNCLE SAM WANTS YOU."

Like so many of Ali's stories, it warrants skepticism, and the irony of the Army recruiting poster is just too perfect in light of his later refusal to be drafted. It seems like one of his too-good-to-be-true stories.

But the impact of Till's murder on his young mind cannot be exaggerated. If he was to make it in the white man's world, he realized, he would have to do it by the white man's rules.

At least until he was big enough to make his own rules.

Boxing was the answer. Boxing kept him strong and healthy. Boxing got him out of his father's house but kept him off the streets. Boxing brought him status and privileges. Boxing imposed a moral, physical, and mental discipline that made it easier to avoid trouble and temptation.

Dope, liquor, girls, gang rumbles, crime, all the pitfalls of the ghetto, could be avoided with a simple "I'm in training to be the champion."

And there was no question that he was. From the age of twelve through eighteen, with a pause of only a few months when he was sidelined with a suspected heart murmur, Cassius devoted himself to becoming the finest amateur boxer in the world. If later on there would be surprising gaps in his worldliness and education, the reason was clear—he had committed himself totally to a narrow path. In six years he fought more than one hundred amateur bouts, losing only a handful, and won most of the country's amateur titles. In Louisville it was assumed he would turn professional after the 1960 Olympics and be managed by William Reynolds of the aluminum family, who had taken an interest in Cassius and hired him as a part-time houseboy at his estate. With such a wealthy sponsor, a rarity for a young boxer, his future seemed assured; no underworld characters would guide him into fixed fights and cheat him out of his earnings.

But Cassius was uneasy about the prospective relationship. He rarely saw Reynolds, and he ate his lunch in the back of the house with the dogs.

5

His
Old Kentucky Home

Cassius returned from Rome to a hero's welcome, parades, testimonial dinners, a handshake from the police chief, a key from the mayor of Louisville, a slap on the back from the governor of Kentucky, who said, "Boy, I know you proud of that name 'Cassius Clay.' I know you proud to carry that name."

Expectedly, contract offers flowed in. Not only had Cassius proven himself a superb boxer at the Olympics, but even more important to managers and promotors, he had proven himself a master of publicity. He was the most photographed, interviewed and talked-about athlete at the Games.

There were solid offers from Patrolman Martin, from Reynolds, the aluminum magnate, from well-known prizefight figures around the country. For one reason or another, Cassius and his father rejected them all. In turn, Cassius was rejected twice when he offered himself to be managed by Joe Louis and by Sugar Ray Robinson, two famous black champions who had been early idols of his. Neither was interested; in fact, both considered him an overrated loudmouth.

Eventually, Clay and his parents signed with the Louisville Sponsoring Group, a local investment club whose only property was Cassius Clay. Made up mostly of Louisville millionaires in the tobacco, whisky, and newspaper aristocracy, the Group gave Clay $10,000 and guaranteed him all training expenses and a modest salary for the next six years in return for fifty cents on every dollar he earned.

It was a very good deal for Cassius, not only for the money (quickly spent to pay off and repair the Clay house and buy Odessa a secondhand pink Cadillac) but for the security of knowing he had six years to carefully develop his talents under top conditions.

As it turned out, of course, it was also a very good deal for the millionaires, who got not only a return on their investment, but an enormous amount of favorable publicity and personal excitement.

Even at the time, Cassius was aware that they perceived him as a sporting property, like their thoroughbred horses and foreign cars, and he was always somewhat annoyed by the press's depiction of them as guardian angels for a poor dumb black boy, and by the general public reaction, best exemplified by the black minister who preached one Sunday that Cassius should "be eternally grateful for what those kind Christian millionaires are doing for his black soul."

But the Louisville Sponsors, even had they wanted to, could not protect Clay from the routine racial discrimination of a city that has never decided whether it is Northern or Southern (during the Civil War, many Kentucky families were torn apart by conflicting Confederate versus Yankee sentiment).

And as Clay so quickly discovered, his cherished Olympic gold medal was no magic amulet for acceptance and recognition in the white world.

Even with the medal on his chest, Clay was refused service in downtown restaurants ("I don't care what he won," said one luncheonette owner; "he's a nigger and he can't eat here"). He was often treated with a contempt that denied his new-found sense of accomplishment. Too many requests for autographs began with the words, "C'mere, boy. . . ."

And then one day the medal disappeared. There has been speculation that the medal was lost or stolen or even pawned by a friend (not such a wild possibility, since years later his professional championship belt was hocked by a member of his entourage).

According to his autobiography, soon after Clay returned to Louisville he and Ronnie King were surrounded by a white motorcycle gang who demanded the Olympic medal in return for safe passage back to his black neighborhood. What followed next reads like a scene out of a low-budget biker movie.

Cassius and Ronnie leaped on their motorbikes and led the gang's big Harley-Davidsons on a grim chase through the side streets and back alleys of Louisville. In a chilling finale of daredevil crashes and some fancy switchblade work by Ronnie, the two young blacks defeated the bikers on the Jefferson County Bridge that links Kentucky and Indiana.

As the bikers slunk back to Louisville, Cassius walked to the center of the bridge, snapped the ribbon that hung around his neck, and hurled the medal into the dark waters of the Ohio.

"Jesus, oh, my God," screamed Ronnie. "Why?"

The answer, as recorded in *The Greatest*, seems just too pat for the eighteen-year-old Cassius Clay to have thought out. But it offers some insight into the sophisticated mind of the thirty-three-year-old Muhammad Ali, who wrote: "I wasn't sure of all the reasons. The Olympic medal had been the most precious thing that had ever come to me. I worshiped it. It was proof of performance, status, a symbol of belonging, of being part of a team, a country, a world. It was my way of redeeming myself with my teachers and schoolmates of Central High, of letting them know that although I had not won scholastic victories, there was something inside of me capable of victory.

"How could I explain to Ronnie I wanted something that meant more than that? Something that was as proud of me as I would be of it. Something that would let me be what I knew I had to be, my own kind of champion."

That was the 1975 version of the medal story, fifteen years after the fact. As an example of "fakelore," it's a clever piece of work; as another irony in Ali's life, it's also almost too perfect.

In 1976, shooting began on a film of Ali's life based

25

loosely on the book. While the filmmakers realized that the biker scene was cinematic dynamite, they did not believe it actually happened.

So they made up their own scene.

The scriptwriter, two-time Academy Award-winner Ring Lardner, Jr., explained: "We decided not to be inhibited by the facts, to change them, if necessary, to adhere to the truth."

In Lardner's "truthful" scene, one of Clay's millionaire owners showed off Cassius and his medal at a Louisville restaurant, but then wouldn't let the young fighter and Ronnie sit and eat with him and his family and friends. Disillusioned, Cassius went to the bridge and threw away his medal.

What really happened to the Olympic medal?

And is what happened really important?

The answer to the second question is for each of us to figure out as we use our own attitudes and intelligences to separate fact from fiction in the life of a man who tends to believe each version of his own story as it is manufactured.

As for the first question, well, we may never know. Ronnie King, who might have known the truth, died in a street fight in 1964, the year Clay became heavyweight champion of the world.

6

The Pro

On October 29, 1960, Cassius Clay won his first professional prizefight, a six-round decision over an experienced older boxer named Tunney Hunsaker, the police chief of a small West Virginia town.

Clay's purse was $2,000, a whopping sum for an eighteen-year-old's pro debut. It was based, of course, on his Olympic fame, and the feeling of many people in the prizefight business that here was a youngster who would make money for them all.

Clay moved to Miami Beach to learn his trade under Angelo Dundee, the same shrewd trainer-manager Clay had called in his hotel room one morning when he was fifteen. The Louisville Group had high hopes for their investment, and could afford the best teacher available.

The association with Dundee would turn out to be

the young fighter's most enduring. In the years to come, Clay would change his name, his religion, his manager, his promotors, and his wives. The faces in his retinue would appear and disappear. His relationship with his father would ebb and flow. But the sad-eyed, quick-tongued little trainer was almost always in his corner. Angelo knew just how to handle him, be he Cassius Clay or Muhammad Ali.

"This is a new kind of person, a new kind of human being," Angelo would tell reporters. "This is a special case where you can't give orders. He doesn't like being yelled at when he works out.

"You tell him what's deficient after a workout. You use the power of suggestion. 'Gee, your left uppercut was working to perfection,' I'll say. He hadn't thrown a left uppercut, but tomorrow he will. This is my easiest job. The guy's a glutton for work. I beg him to take a day off."

An Italian-American born Angelo Mirena and raised in Philadelphia, Dundee had just the right combination of street smarts and boxing savvy and child psychology to help an immature, egocentric black teenager who was brilliantly creative in the ring but often lost outside it. (The Scottish name, Dundee, was first adopted by an older brother who, like many Italian and Jewish fighters of the 1930's and 1940's, fought under pseudonyms so their mothers would not know—perhaps that's one reason why Angelo was never as upset as so many others when Cassius changed his name.)

The admiration was mutual. Of Dundee, Clay said:

"He'll listen to whatever you want to say. He considers how his fighters feel. There ain't never no boss between me and Angelo. We discuss things on a sensible basis. I've never seen Angelo really mad, arguing, fussing. He's always jolly and playful. We have lots of fun together. Plus a lot of places he can go with me"— Clay would wink, tapping the swarthy skin of Angelo's arm—"because he's half colored."

Angelo carefully avoided any involvement in Clay's private life. He was probably among the first white men to know that the young fighter was attending meetings of the black separatist sect then called the Lost-Found Nation of Islam, but he shrugged off questions and said nothing to Clay. As far as Angelo was concerned, the relationship was bounded by the ring ropes. He might help Cassius write his poetry, laugh too hard at his jokes, even feign terror when Cassius jumped out of a hotel room closet shouting "BOO!" but he never offered personal advice. His job as he saw it was to condition Cassius' body, refine his boxing style, and keep him in "the best mental frame of mind."

In the early pro years, at least, the job was fun. Most trainers complain that their most difficult tasks are to wake up their boxers in the morning, get them out running before dawn, cajole them into the gym for workouts, and get them back into bed early, and alone. In other words, to make them train.

But Cassius loved to run and loved to spar and loved to condition his body. Clay's vanity has always bordered on narcissism, and the sight of a softening muscle or a roll of flesh around his midsection would drive him to a frenzy of calisthenics—a good thing, too, because Clay, and later Ali, was a prodigious eater with a weakness for ice cream and other sweets, and a tendency to put on weight.

Ali is so vain about his body, in fact, that he has been known to spar before audiences without wearing the cumbersome metal-and-leather protective harness under his trunks that all fighters wear as a matter of course. Always self-conscious about his big backside, Ali feels that the harness makes his rump look even bigger and "spoils the line" of his figure.

Outside Angelo Dundee's Fifth Street Gym in Miami Beach, despite all his talk of tomato-red limousines and "foxes" (his word for pretty girls), Clay was no late-night carouser. His sidekick in those years was Howard Bingham, a Los Angeles photographer who still remains a close friend. Bingham first met Clay in 1962.

"He was always a little shy with girls," says Bingham. "Believe it or not, he could get tongue-tied if he had to ask for a date. Oh, he was great kidding around, or boasting, but he was no fast-talker and no matter what people say now, he never had a lot of girl friends in those days."

He was, and still is, most comfortable with children. "The only difference between me and the Pied Piper," he liked to say, "is the Pied Piper didn't have no Cadillac."

Pleasant, courteous, respectful of older people, Cassius in private life was a distinct contrast to the howling braggart of his public image, the publicity hound who wrote:

Me
Wheeeeeeeeeeee!

and then added, "I'm a very modest person."

There were other paradoxes evident in the early 1960's that are still in his personality. For all the supposed savagery of the prize ring, he has always been somewhat squeamish about violence.

He will rarely batter an injured opponent (critics call that a lack of "killer instinct"), and he rarely goes for the brain-jarring knockouts that come from heavy head slugging. He seems to prefer winning by decision, by one-punch knockouts of weary opponents ready to drop, or by the technical knockouts called by referees who stop the fight when one man is either bleeding badly or clearly outclassed.

This is not entirely humanitarian behavior—even more than hurting others he dislikes being hurt himself.

He had played football once as a child, but gave it up when someone tackled him hard.

"They gave me the ball and tackled me," he said. "My helmet hit the ground. POW! No sir. You got to get hit in that game. Toooooo rough. You don't have to get hit in boxing. People don't understand that."

His own boxing style has always reflected an unwillingness to expose himself to getting hit. Most heavyweights are willing to take a few hard punches for the chance to give some, especially sluggers like Joe

Frazier who have more endurance than skill. But Clay had enormous talent, he had a face he liked just the way it was, and he knew that every punch that hit him would take a little more time off his boxing life.

His fighting speed was always dazzling, but as he matured into a six-foot-three-inch panther he became physically intimidating. He had always been faster than most of his opponents, but now he was bigger as well, a devastating combination. Boxing experts sneered at his unorthodox style—he held his hands too low, they said, he rested against the ropes too much, he still was leaning backward instead of sideways to avoid punches—but Angelo defended it: "He's an individualist, he's doing what's right for him."

He certainly was. Two years after his first pro fight, Clay had registered sixteen straight victories, all but three by knockout. Angelo, of course, was "bringing him along carefully," which is boxing talk for matching a young fighter against opponents who will help him develop skills and self-confidence without exactly endangering his career; but Cassius still had to fight alone in the ring against large men who could hurt or beat him.

By the time he was twenty years old, he had earned $100,000 as a fighter. He bought his parents a new home, in a Louisville suburb, and he bought himself a black Cadillac limousine and an old bus, on which he had painted CASSIUS CLAY, THE WORLD'S MOST COLORFUL FIGHTER.

7

The Contender

Skeptics doubted his boxing talent, but no one doubted his genius for self-promotion. The Group was buying him time and training. Angelo was steering his career. But it was Cassius who made himself a box-office smash.

There was endless doggerel:

> *This is the story about a man*
> *With iron fists and beautiful tan.*
> *He talks a lot and boasts indeed*
> *Of a power punch and blinding speed.*

There was an incredible lack of traditional athletic humility:

"I am beautiful. Beeeoootiful. I'm the greatest, I'm the double-greatest. I am clean and sparkling. I will be a clean and sparkling champion."

And there were those uncanny predictions:

Archie's been living off the fat of the land—
I'm here to give him his pension plan.
When you come to the fight don't block the door,
'Cause you'll all go home after Round Four.

After his sixteenth pro fight, on November 15, 1962, in which he did indeed knock out the old ex-champion light heavyweight Archie Moore in the fourth round, Clay became the hottest property in boxing.

"The Louisville Lip," as the sportswriters called him, couldn't have happened along at a better time.

Boxing was in worse shape than usual.

In contrast to every other major professional sport in America, boxing has never had a strong legal central government. There is no national commissioner, no leagues, no logical sequence of bouts, no system to assure a fighter success in accord with his ability. There is no welfare or pension program to protect the old or sick boxer, no nationwide medical and safety standards.

There is not even a national set of rules! This is why the weight of the gloves, the size of the ring, even the method of scoring rounds, can vary from fight to fight. It's as if the size of the baseball, the distance to first base, and the number of balls and strikes were changed for every baseball game.

Traditionally, this anarchistic sport looked to the underworld for financial support and for policing. Legitimate businessmen were wary about risking their money and their reputations in this often-crooked game. Enter the racketeers. Not only did they have unaccounted cash to spend and no reputations to lose, they had the muscle to discipline rough, slum-bred fighters, bookies, fixers, and anyone else who got out of line.

But the sport changed drastically just before Cassius Clay entered the scene. First of all, a big court decision broke up the International Boxing Club, a shady syndicate of millionaires, known gangsters, and powerful promotors known to their enemies as "Octopus, Inc." Madison Square Garden, once the capital of boxing, lost its monopoly.

Second of all, at about the same time, an electronic process was perfected by which closed-circuit telecasts could be beamed to theaters around the world. Regular home television had overexposed boxing, and people were now interested in big entertainments such as championship shows rather than weekly club fights.

The beneficiary of all these changes should have been Floyd Patterson, a moody, introspective young black champion who had never been part of the gangster regime. In fact, his wily manager, Cus D'Amato, had been one of the Octopus' most implacable foes. But Floyd didn't have the temperament to relax and enjoy his title. He hungered for universal acceptance as the greatest champion of all. And this meant fighting the one man that Cus begged him to avoid, a brutal ex-convict with baleful eyes, the seemingly invincible Sonny Liston.

Although Sonny was also a black man, Negro activist groups, liberal commentators, even President

Kennedy and his family, were afraid that he would set back civil rights progress if he became champion. Patterson was intelligent, sensitive, honorable, the kind of positive black role model that people in the rights movement felt helped their cause. Liston was considered just a thug who could hit like a mule.

The more people begged Floyd to duck Sonny's challenge, the more determined Floyd was to prove himself a true champion by conquering the brute.

Patterson and Liston fought twice, in 1962 and in 1963. Each time, Sonny knocked out Floyd in the very first round.

And so the call went out for a handsome young fighter to rescue the heavyweight crown, to snatch it away from the monster and bring it back to decency and light.

Guess who accepted?

Cassius Clay now set his course for a championship collision with the new heavyweight king, Sonny Liston.

Naturally, Cassius did it his way.

In January of 1963, at the weigh-in for a fight with a tough, competent slugger named Charlie Powell, Clay appeared to go crazy. At the scale he challenged Powell to fight and started screaming, "You wait and see, you'll go in three."

Sportswriters, not realizing it was a carefully rehearsed act calculated to upset Powell and boost last-minute ticket sales, wrote that Clay had to be "restrained" by his seconds. They wrote that he was hysterical and scared. They called him "Gaseous Cassius."

And then they had to eat their words when he knocked out Powell in the third round, as promised.

In March, in Madison Square Garden, he faced Doug Jones, who was considered his best opponent so far. Jones was strong and stumpy and he never stopped boring in on Clay's stand-up, lean-back, jab-and-dance style. Many people who saw that fight think Jones won it, that the referee and judges gave it to Clay because he was unbeaten and the boxing world's hope for the future. When the ten-round decision was announced in Clay's favor, the audience booed and hurled trash at the ring.

But the next week, Cassius's picture appeared on the cover of *Time* magazine, an uncommon honor in those days for a black athlete who had just recently turned twenty-one.

In June, Cassius flew to London and fought Henry Cooper, the British champion. Cassius stopped traffic in Picadilly Circus, strutting around in bowler and morning coat. He sold out the arena with his cry, "This is no jive, Cooper will go in five."

There have always been arguments about Clay's ability to predict the "round in which the clown will fall to the ground," as he put it. Some people suspected fixed fights.

But the best explanation was in his consummate superiority to most of his opponents, his ability to so control, even choreograph, a fight that he could actually decide when he wanted to knock out an opponent. He might do this either by "carrying" a weak fighter, which meant he would let up the attack whenever the opponent seemed about to fall, or by mounting a sudden, irresistable assault on a strong fighter. Many knockouts are as psychological as they are physical; faced with a determined attacker who just won't quit throwing punishing blows, many a fighter has gratefully gone down long before he could be knocked "out."

As for those predictions, people only recalled the ones that came true. They tended to forget, for example, that Doug Jones was supposed to "meet his fate in eight unless I get sore, then he'll go in four."

To anyone who would listen, Clay would confide the secret of his promotional brilliance: He had learned to boast and prance from observing Gorgeous George, the blondined wrestler of the Fifties who filled arenas with screaming people who wanted to see him shut up for good.

That July of 1963, Liston demolished Patterson a second time. There were no other challengers on the horizon with the box-office appeal to take advantage of the new closed-circuit television technology in a championship bout with Liston. Even though almost everyone believed that Clay would not only lose, but be badly hurt, the stage was set for a Liston-Clay million-dollar extravaganza.

"I want that big ugly bear," screamed Clay.

Liston replied, "I'll get locked up for murder if I fight him."

8

The Beatles and Malcolm X

For all the certainty that Liston would destroy Clay, there was no real outcry against the "mismatch." When I was sent down to cover the fight for *The New York Times*, I was instructed to check out the location of the nearest hospital so I wouldn't waste valuable deadline time following Cassius to intensive care.

But there were no outraged editorials demanding cancellation of the bout. Perhaps after the examples of Jack Dempsey, Joe Louis, and Rocky Marciano—tigers in the ring but modest, humble men outside it—SportsWorld really wanted "The Mighty Mouth" silenced.

The buildup to the fight was a spectacle in itself. One day the Beatles, on their first American tour, visited Clay at his training gym. Although they had never met before, they all climbed into the ring and fell into a hilarious comedy routine that looked as though it had been rehearsed for days. John and Ringo and Paul and George fell down like dominoes and popped up like jacks-in-the-box as Cassius pretended to beat them up. Whether or not he could beat Liston, everyone agreed that Cassius was a championship clown.

An international press corps of more than five hundred descended on Miami Beach, including such literary heavyweights as Norman Mailer and Budd Schulberg. When Clay's assistant trainer, Drew (Bundini) Brown, created the battle cry "Float like a butterfly, sting like a bee, rumble, young man, rumble," it was transmitted around the world and translated into dozens of languages.

Las Vegas odds makers established Liston as a seven-to-one favorite, and the surly champion growled, "If that little baby even dreamed of beating me he'd apologize. I'm going to spank him."

There was even a subplot of mystery and dread in the circus atmosphere that enveloped the fight camps before the big bout. Rumors had been building for some months that Cassius had formally joined the Lost-Found Nation of Islam, called the Black Muslims by the white press, and that he had even taken the name Cassius X to show that he had discarded the "slave name" of Clay, given to his ancestors by the white plantation masters.

Now, in February of 1964, when it was learned that the fiery prime minister of the Black Muslims, the famous Malcolm X, was a guest of Cassius' in Miami, there was no question that the rumor was true. Cassius was on the verge of renouncing his Christian religion. His brother, Rudy, who followed him in most things, had already become a Muslim. Clay, it was assumed, was waiting to announce his conversion until after the fight—it would have more impact if he won.

In those days of intense feeling about civil rights for black Americans, the Nation of Islam was looked upon as a dangerous group. It had been formed by a former Georgia sharecropper named Elijah Poole who claimed to have been visited by Allah. He now called himself the Messenger of Allah, the Honorable Elijah Muhammad, and he drew his adherents from poor neighborhoods and from jails. He forbade them to drink, smoke, eat pork products, dance, or use drugs. He encouraged them to build strong family relationships and operate their own businesses. While the ministers of other religions for black people taught them they were as good as whites, Elijah taught his people that they were better, and that when Judgment Day came the "blue-eyed white devils" would be destroyed. He urged them to have as little to do with whites as possible.

It might have been just another ghetto cult without Malcolm X, a brilliant, energetic former convict who became one of Elijah's chief spokesmen, and one of America's most important black voices. Only a few months before the scheduled Clay-Liston fight, in November 1963, Malcolm characterized the murder of President Kennedy as "chickens coming home to roost." Violence, Malcolm was saying, only breeds more violence.

41

Despite the ballyhoo and the intrigue, Clay was remarkably calm in the days before the fight. He might have been the only person who was *sure* he was going to win.

Late one afternoon, after he had finished his public workout, he stretched out on a rubbing table, his chin propped on his fists, smiling at himself in a locker-room mirror. "You are so beautiful," he said.

The steam from open shower stalls fogged the mirror and curled the notebook pages of journalists who had crowded in to interview him.

"But what if you lose, Cassius, what happens then?" asked a columnist from Los Angeles.

"So beautiful," he said as his image faded in the steam. "Your publicity has overshadowed your talent. You are the double-greatest."

"Let's be serious for a minute," insisted a sportswriter from Boston. "What if the champ beats you?"

Cassius laughed into his fists. "I won't feel bad. I'll have tricked all the people into coming to the fight, to paying two hundred and fifty dollars for a ticket when they wouldn't have paid one hundred dollars without my talk."

"So this whole act," said the Boston man, "is just a con job, eh?"

"People ain't gonna give you nothing no way. You gotta go get it." He pushed himself up on the table, and his eyes sparkled. "I'm making all this money, the popcorn man making money and the beer man, and you got something to write about. Your papers let you come down to Miami Beach where it's warm."

The Boston man seemed a little angry at that. Sportswriters don't like to be reminded that without athletes to write about they wouldn't exist. "Exactly what are you going to do when Sonny Liston beats you after all your big talk?"

"If Liston beats me, the next day I'll be on the sidewalk hollering 'No man ever beat me twice.' I'll be screaming for a rematch."

The big brown body relaxed and seemed to melt into the rubbing table. The voice dropped to a whisper.

"Or maybe I'll quit the ring for good. I'm twenty-two years old now." He closed his eyes. "I think I'm getting tired of fighting."

9

The Champion

Right up until the moment Cassius stepped into the ring, rumors were flying that he had left the country. At the weigh-in that morning of February 25, 1964, Cassius topped his Charlie Powell performance with a mad scene that left him practically foaming. He ranted and raged, he challenged Liston to fight him at the scales, and again he had to be "restrained" by his friends.

Liston was convinced Clay was crazy, and a local boxing commission doctor reported that his pulse was an abnormally high 120 because Clay was "scared to death." The press generally accepted the medical opinion, and when Cassius was not in his dressing room an hour before the fight they assumed he was either in shock or on a plane.

Actually, he was standing very quietly in a corner

of the arena watching his brother, Rudy, win his very first professional fight. Then Cassius dressed for his own date with destiny, his twentieth professional fight.

It was finally time to put his fists where his mouth had been.

Clay was in control from the opening bell, dancing away from Sonny Liston's vaunted left hook, then leaping in to deliver quick barrages to Liston's head. He opened a nasty gash under Liston's left eye in the third round. Later, six stitches were required to close the wound.

The crowd was flabbergasted. It had barely gotten over the first shock of discovering that David was about three inches taller than Goliath, and considerably broader, when they realized that the loudmouthed braggart had been telling the truth all along—he was obviously unafraid of the monster, and a far better boxer.

Clay was in trouble only once. Seconds before the bell sounded for the fifth round to begin, Cassius' eyes began to burn. Much later he would learn that the liniment Liston's cornermen had been slathering on the champion's sore shoulder had somehow gotten from Liston's gloves to Clay's forehead and then dripped down into Clay's eyes.

In the heat of battle, Clay was sure that his eyes were stinging with a poison that was blinding him. He wanted to quit before he was permanently hurt. He screamed to Angelo Dundee to stop the fight.

"Cut the gloves off!"

"Daddy, this is the big one," snapped cool Angelo.

"This is for the title. Get in there."

At the bell, he shoved Cassius out to the center of the ring.

Blinking, stumbling, Cassius avoided Liston for the first minute of the round. Several times he stretched out his left glove to touch Liston's nose and keep the champion at arm's length. Toward the end of the round his vision cleared. His confidence returned and he went back to the attack.

Liston never came out for the seventh round. He remained on his stool, slumped, as the referee raised Clay's hand in triumph. Liston's left arm hung uselessly at his side; he had torn muscles in his left shoulder swinging at and missing his elusive target.

Reporters at ringside were still trying to figure out the bizarre ending when the new champion shouted down from the ring apron, "EAT YOUR WORDS. I AM THE GREATEST. I . . . AM . . . THE . . . GREATEST."

10

The Muslim

"I'm through talking," said the new heavyweight champion of the world. "All I have to do is to be a nice, clean gentleman."

At his press conference the next morning, Clay was so unusually soft-spoken that we had to strain to hear him. He recapitulated the fight in such an objective way, so reasonably promised to defend his new title against all ranking contenders, and displayed such patience and poise that most reporters left quickly to file sympathetic stories about "a new Clay molded to the championship throne."

Only a handful of us remained when someone asked him if he was a "card-carrying member of the Black Muslims." In those days, the phrase "card-carrying member" usually referred to bomb-throwing revolutionaries, and was not to be used lightly.

"Card-carrying, what does that mean?" snapped Clay, his eyes suddenly hard. "I go to a Black Muslim meeting and what do I see? I see there's no smoking and no drinking and no fornicating and their women wear dresses down to the floor. And then I come out on the street and you tell me I shouldn't go in there. Well, there must be something in there if you don't want me to go."

His voice became sharper as he parried more questions. He was asked about the civil rights movement. "Who needs it?" he answered. "I'm a citizen already."

He was asked about Malcolm X, with whom he had eaten vanilla ice cream the night before at his victory party.

"If he's so bad," asked Clay, "why don't they put him in jail?"

He was asked about being a Muslim. Was he now Cassius X?

"I catch so much hell. Why? Why me, when I don't try to bust into schools or march around or throw bricks?"

He was referring, of course, to efforts by many blacks and whites to integrate schools and public transportation and other facilities by picketing and demonstrations. Since he seemed to be parroting the segregationist line, several liberal white reporters tried to argue with him. But he silenced them.

"Listen! In the jungle the lions are with lions, and the tigers with tigers, and redbirds stay with redbirds and bluebirds with bluebirds. That's human nature,

48

too, to be with your own kind. I don't want to go where I'm not wanted."

A reporter mentioned the responsibility of the heavyweight champion to be a model for young people. Clay replied calmly that he wanted to be nice to everyone, but no one would make him into something he was not.

"I know where I'm going and I know the truth and I don't have to be what you want me to be. I'm free to be who I want."

A very simple statement, but at that time, coming from a young heavyweight champion, it was profound and revolutionary.

Free to be who I want.

It was a declaration of independence from traditional SportsWorld, from the way America had treated its young black athletes. In time, those words would have even greater significance, but they were powerful enough right then.

Contrary to custom, the new champion was not invited to the White House. And the only black leader to send Cassius Clay a congratulatory telegram was the Reverend Martin Luther King, Jr.

11

Enter Muhammad Ali

In mellow moments before he won the heavyweight title, Cassius Clay had a recurring fantasy he loved to dream out loud. It went like this:

"When I get that championship I'm gonna put on my old jeans and get an old hat and grow a beard and I'm gonna walk down an old country road where nobody knows me till I find a pretty little fox who don't know my name, who just loves me for what I am.

"And then I'll take her back to my $250,000 house overlooking my $1,000,000 housing development and I'll show her all my Cadillacs and the indoor pool in case it rains and I'll tell her, 'This is yours, honey, 'cause you love me for what I am.' "

It was a very standard male fantasy for someone raised in the Fifties, that decade when dollars and dreams got all mixed up. It was about love and money, about measuring oneself through possessions, but being afraid that a woman might want you more for what you owned than what you were.

It was such a standard fantasy, in fact, that many people were shocked by what Cassius Clay did in the months immediately after he won the title.

He renounced his Christian religion and, indirectly, the upbringing of his parents. He gave up millions of dollars in record, movie, and endorsement contracts offered to him as the most photogenic fighter in history. He denounced the movement toward integration. He married an older woman with a child by a previous marriage. And to cap it all, he took a new name, one bestowed upon him by the Honorable Elijah.

Muhammad Ali, he proudly announced, meant "Worthy of all praise most high."

He had left behind, he said, his former self, "Cassius Clay the Clown," to become "Muhammad Ali the Wise Man."

The white press attacked him. For those who had cherished the ebullient, patriotic Cassius of Rome, this new, unsmiling, dogmatic Ali was an enigma and a betrayer.

He was considered "ungrateful" to the American Way of Life that had made him rich and famous.

His avowed rebirth in a new religion was considered "misguided."

And, worst crime of all to his critics, he was no longer entertaining. Instead of spouting lighthearted verse he was now offering undigested lumps of unpopular ideology that forced people to think.

"It's natural that the American Negro should have a Muslim nature," he said. "Those bombings, and they never caught the people who did it. The Civil Rights Bill having all that trouble, and all those people talking so it don't come to a vote, and Kennedy did so much for the Negro and he died. Things die out and our people forget. Three hundred and ten years of physical slavery, the faithful slave I see on a corner in Harlem and he has to ask for a dollar 'cause he's hungry.

"All our lives we learn that black is evil, it's dirty, they even call black cake devil's food cake, and now we learn in our Muslim temples that the richest dirt and the strongest coffee is black. So Muslim fits us like a glove."

Few people, white or black, could understand how a handsome healthy black man would voluntarily give up the glamorous high life so accessible to an American sports hero.

Some people thought that Ali had been "brainwashed" by Malcolm X. There were rumors that the Muslims had a "death-threat hold" on the young boxer (and, of course, that Liston had dumped the fight rather than risk being rubbed out by a Muslim "death squad").

Very few people wanted to think about the possibility that Ali was sincere; that the Muslim minister who had originally "fished" the seventeen-year-old Cassius Clay off a street corner with talk of "the blue-eyed white devil" was casting with a lure that had great meaning for the young boxer.

At the mosque, Cassius was entranced by the cleanliness of the Muslims, their dietary laws, the purity of their women, and the sense of belonging he could feel in the brotherhood of quiet, responsible family men.

For a boxer in serious training, Muslim rules were easy to follow; he was not one to drink or smoke or take drugs or carouse all night anyway.

For a man who had never been completely relaxed in the presence of women, the laws provided a certain protection; they were even better than the "I'm in training to be the champion" explanation that had helped insulate his youth.

The message of black superiority was a balm on all the racial wounds and fears of his youth, and the pseudointellectual Muslim teachings were heady stuff for one whose high-school diploma had practically been a gift for his athletic achievements.

Ali had never forgiven the black preacher who had told him to "be eternally grateful" to the kind white Christian millionaires, and now he could hear Black Muslim preachers deride the "spooks and ghosts" of his former religion as white men's tricks to enslave the black man on earth with a promise of "pie in the sky when you die by and by."

The Muslims told their followers to get theirs "down on the ground while you're still around."

There is no way to measure the depth of a religious experience, nor to what extent a believer finds in his religion just those attributes he wants to find. Cassius did not become a Muslim at seventeen, when he was first introduced to the religion, but he flirted with the idea for years as he investigated other religions, looking for a peace and order in his world, a shield from hurt, a greater truth through divinity, a mythology, a new language, a surrogate family. By the time he became an active Muslim at twenty-two, he thought he had found what he needed.

With the zealousness of the convert, Ali became a super-Muslim. It was the teachings of the Honorable Elijah, he would say, that enabled him to become heavyweight champion. As a champion, he said, he had a responsibility to provide a model for black youth.

Unlike most athletic stars, he spent time in the ghettoes, walking the "little streets filled with little people." He shook hands with the wino, he said, because this would give the wretched man a measure of self-respect: If he, the champ, shrank from a wino as everyone else did, the man would just curl deeper into resentment and hopelessness. Of course, basic to this attitude was Ali's feeling of superiority to the wino.

Wherever Ali went, he brought the Muslim message of "straighten up and fly right" that owes more to the puritan ethic than to the mysticism of the East. Years later, Ali would say that this hard-line, no-frills, anti-white ideology was the first step in Elijah's master plan, given to him by Allah, to clean up the American black for eventual integration with white society on an equal level: Before the black people could take their rightful place they had to have individual and racial pride.

But the bubbly Cassius Clay was never completely submerged in the new hard-line Muhammad Ali. The summer after he won the title, I was riding through Harlem with him in his chauffeur-driven limousine. He was speaking like a pompous elder statesman about his recent tour of Africa and the Middle East as an ambassador of the American branch of Islam, when his eyes suddenly lit up.

"Hey, you know what happened on the way to Egypt? I sat with the pilot, that's right, the pilot of a big jet plane, and he talked to me about boxing while he drove the plane, and I sat behind a wheel, too, and whenever he turned his wheel, my wheel turned, too, and I could sit there and pretend I was driving the plane."

He talked faster, louder. "Then it was time to land, and that's a crucial time, and I stayed in the pilot's room, but went to another seat, and I was there, right there when we landed, in a place where most people don't even get a chance to *peek.*"

He flicked on the limo's record player and began clapping his hands and bobbing his head to the rocking beat of a current hit song, "What's the Matter with You, Baby?" pounding his knee to the rhythm, sometimes shouting snatches of lyric out the window at pretty girls along the street.

He ordered the driver to take us to the Muslims' Temple No. 7 restaurant, where we all piled out and, at Ali's urging—"It's good, man, it is gooooood"— sampled the sweet, dense navy-bean pie.

As he shoveled in the food, Ali checked out the attractive young waitresses in their flowing white dresses.

"When I get married," he whispered, "it's gonna be to a pretty little Muslim girl, seventeen years old, I can teach her my ways. A virgin, a girl ain't no one touched."

Yet a few months later he married Sonji Roi, a beautiful cocktail waitress and model from Chicago. She was several years older than Ali, worldly, and independent. She had been on her own since she was fifteen years old. She had been married before; she had a child.

Herbert Muhammad, a son of Elijah, had introduced them. He had warned Ali, "Have a nice time but don't get serious." But the young champion fell hard. She was the first woman he had ever loved, he admitted later; she was also, probably, the first woman with whom he had had a sustained physical relationship.

The marriage was doomed from the start.

Sonji smoked, drank, wore cosmetics, loved to dance and party. She wore short skirts and revealing blouses. Most significant, she had a mind of her own. While she was willing to attend Muslim meetings, she questioned the teachings. Ali was still too new in the religion to explain away the inconsistencies between Muslim doctrine and practice that a bright, street-wise woman like Sonji would wave in his face.

They squabbled over religion, food, money, clothes. Once, Ali nearly got into a fistfight with his old idol Sugar Ray Robinson. Sonji wore a particularly low-cut dress to a party given by Sugar Ray, and Ali, arriving later, got angry and almost ripped it off her. Sugar Ray objected to Ali's treatment of his wife, and only the intercession of other guests prevented the two fighters from squaring off.

Later, Ali would admit that he was probably too immature for marriage at twenty-two, especially after spending most of his life between twelve and twenty-two in a boxing gym.

In an unusual tape-recorded dialogue with Ali that was reprinted in *The Greatest*, Sonji had this to say: "Some of my close girl friends would come up and say, 'Baby, I'd wear a fisherman's net under a deep-sea diver's suit, with a Ku Klux Klan sheet and a monk's frock if I had a husband that rich and handsome and famous, and he dug me wearing it.'

"They didn't understand. It wasn't the form of the thing. But simply to tell me 'believe' or 'not to do' something—that's different, even though I always want to obey my husband and I'll do anything to make him happy. Having a Messenger of God over him . . . this thing of having someone above my own man, as his leader and teacher . . . I could never accept making another man happy outside of my husband. I wanted no man to tell my husband what to make me do. I wanted only my husband to be the final word."

They remained together, off and on, for less than a year. The marriage lasted as long as it did only because Ali did not want to face the pain of separation until after he had faced Sonny Liston again. Originally, the rematch between them was scheduled for November 16, 1964, in Boston, but just a few days before the fight Ali was rushed to the hospital for emergency surgery for a hernia. (Liston, with characteristic sympathy, quipped, "He been opening his mouth so much he let too much air in").

The fight was rescheduled for May 25, 1965, in the small, depressed mill town of Lewiston, Maine. Boston politicians had decided they didn't want the fight in their city after all: too many problems, too great a risk of an ugly incident that might cause bad publicity for Boston.

First of all, there was the chance, the politicians thought, that the fight might be crooked. Liston was mixed up with the underworld, or at least had been earlier in his career. A fixed fight would give Boston a black eye as a sporting city.

Second, there was the chance that pickets and boycotters and other demonstrators angry at Ali for joining the Black Muslims might make the fight a flop. Ali was getting more and more negative publicity in newspapers and on television, and Boston politicians were afraid of giving the impression that they condoned his joining the unpopular group.

Third, there was the chance that Ali would be assassinated in the ring.

Malcolm X, Ali's original Muslim mentor, had left the group in a bitter dispute with Elijah over the aims of the sect. He had set up his own organization. On February 21, 1965, he was shot to death in New York. That night there was a mysterious fire in Ali's Chicago apartment while he and Sonji were out to dinner. It was widely assumed that Muslims had killed Malcolm and that it was only a matter of time before Malcolm's followers avenged his death by killing the Muslims' new superstar, Muhammad Ali.

In Lewiston, the champion was constantly surrounded by tough, hard-eyed Fruit of Islam, the Muslims' karate-trained security force. They became even more protective of the champion when a report circulated that a carload of gunmen was en route from New York.

Reporters, particularly those assigned ringside seats near Ali's corner, were nervous. One of the promotors took out a one-night million-dollar insurance policy on Ali's life. He did it for the publicity, cynically figuring that many people would buy tickets to the closed-circuit television show in hopes of seeing a live assassination.

Only the fighters seemed unconcerned. Ali, quite rightly, assumed that the killer-car story was all part of a plot to upset him. And Liston shrugged and said, "Why should I worry—they're coming to get him, not me, right?"

Had there been snipers in that Maine hockey arena, they would have had to work very fast. Barely had the crowd settled down for the first round when Liston was flat on his stomach, his face pressed to the canvas. Even the referee, former champion Jersey Joe Walcott, was stunned. He lost track of the count. People in the crowd yelled, "Fix!" and reporters described the knockout blow as "The Phantom Punch."

Actually, it was "The Perfect Punch." The fighters were moving toward each other at top speed, each throwing his weight of more than two hundred pounds behind a potential knockout punch.

Liston's, a left, missed.

Ali's, a short right thrown on a downward arc, smashed into the left side of Liston's face. The challenger collapsed slowly, like a building crumbling during an earthquake.

Once again Ali was on the ring apron, taunting the predominantly hostile press. "Will there ever be another like me?"

As far as most of the reporters were concerned, one like him was more than enough. No one likes to be reminded of mistakes, and the sportswriters had stubbornly maintained that Ali was a fluke champion soon to be deposed. They couldn't believe that someone so different from the heroes they had been taught—and, in turn, had taught others—to admire could be such a great athlete.

And they were stuck with him, too. The sports press had helped build up Cassius Clay and now, for better or worse, it had to cover Muhammad Ali.

Until he lost his title, that is.

And so, the call went out again for a man to save boxing. Floyd Patterson was delighted to be resurrected. He was the "White Hope." But Patterson went a little too far for his own good when he declared:

"The image of a Black Muslim as the heavyweight champion disgraces the sport and the nation. Cassius Clay must be beaten and the Black Muslims' scourge removed from boxing."

12

A Time Out

That summer of 1965, in an attempt to clear his mind and raise his spirits, Ali made an exhibition tour of Europe. He needed to get away and think, to meet new people. He had successfully defended his championship, he had beaten Liston twice, and things had just gotten worse for him.

Separating from Sonji had been even more painful than he had thought; he was truly torn between his religion and the woman he loved. His popularity with the sports press and the white establishment had been further diminished by the unpleasant atmosphere of the Lewiston fight and its abrupt and suspect ending. He began to see the shape of things to come—his government and his fellow citizens were turning against him.

There was no solace in Europe. In fact, in Stockholm he ran into a new—and ludicrous—area of controversy. The Swedish reporters, from Communist to right wing, were irked by his lack of interest in their women. Every other black fighter who ever toured Scandinavia had dated the local blondes. Floyd Patterson even married one.

Angelo Dundee spent a frantic day explaining to reporters that there was nothing anti-Swedish in Ali's indifference, it was merely a tenet of his religion. But headlines the next day blew the story into something approaching a racial slur. Ali was *anti-Swede*.

At his exhibition match in a large amusement park, the crowd seemed bored by his poems and his sparring. When he started to make a speech, they interrupted with the chant, "We want Floyd. We want Floyd."

Back in his hotel, Ali seemed unusually moody. He was tired and depressed. He had always recharged his psychic battery with the energy of crowds, and the Swedes had left his battery dead. He threw himself onto his bed. I took a chair.

"Man, you just can't go strong all the time," he murmured into his pillow. "Can't be such a controversial figure, dodging all the traps. . . ."

He suddenly looked up at me. "Why do I catch all this hell? I don't drink or smoke or chase bad women. I treat everybody nice."

I shrugged. I had no answer for him then.

"You know," he said, "nobody ever came up to me and said, 'I'm going to become a Muslim because you are.' You have to live it and practice it and sacrifice and study.

"You don't love the cereal because Willie Mays eats it, but you might try it because of the man. But then you got to go and do the thing yourself."

13

Punishing Floyd

Floyd Patterson, a good fighter and a decent man, was still so hungry for the fame and glory that Sonny Liston had twice knocked out of his grasp that he allowed himself to be promoted not only as Muhammad Ali's opponent in the ring but as the patriotic, Christian hero who was going to "give the title back to America."

Patterson went along with every conceivable attack on Ali. He put down Ali's religion, calling the Muslims a hate group and Elijah a fraud. He described Ali as a misguided fool for finding a sense of roots in the Third World ("I'm not no American," said Ali after a trip to Africa; "I'm a black man"). He expressed the fear of white boxing businessmen that the Muslims would "take over" the sport and squeeze them out.

And he was always careful to call Muhammad Ali

by the name he had renounced, Cassius Clay.

Before their fight, which was held in Las Vegas coincidentally on the second anniversary of President Kennedy's assassination, November 22, 1965, Muhammad Ali avoided engaging in an ideological war with Floyd.

"I'm certainly not going to attack his religion," Ali would say. "How can I attack all these Catholic people, the Pope, and those wonderful people who run hospitals and help little children, why should I attack them for the sake of one fool?"

Ali saved all his anger for the fight. Like a little boy pulling off the wings of a butterfly piecemeal, he mocked and humiliated and punished Patterson for almost twelve rounds, until the referee threw his body in front of Patterson to protect the defenseless challenger.

Later, Patterson would say he couldn't fight back because a chronic back injury had flared up to cripple him. And critics of Ali maintained that Ali had tried to knock out Patterson, but failed.

More objective observers believed that Ali had had no intention of polishing off Patterson quickly, that he had planned to keep him in misery as long as possible. From the beginning, Ali picked Patterson's face apart with snake-lick jabs, backing off whenever Floyd seemed ready to collapse.

And he taunted him continuously: "No contest, get me a contender. . . . Boop, boop, boop. . . . Watch out, Floyd. . . . Bang."

It was the fulfillment of his prediction that he would

"chastise" Floyd for his remarks, for refusing to call him Muhammad Ali. It was an ugly, sickening exhibition. It was as if he accepted Floyd as the symbol of all the people who were criticizing him, the media, the politicians, the civil rights leaders, the boxing officials, and punished them all through Floyd.

After the fight, he punished them some more, although this time with sly and subtle words. At a press conference he told Patterson: "Floyd, you should get honors and medals, the spot you was on, a good, clean American boy fighting for America. All those movie stars behind you, they should make sure you never have to work another day in your life. It would be a disgrace on the government if you had to end up scuffling somewhere."

Floyd swallowed it. "I was beaten by a great fighter, Muhammad Ali," he said, using the hated name for the first time.

That name. In 1965, the media choked on the name. The closest most publications would come to acknowledging it was to refer to the champion as "Cassius Clay, who prefers to be called Muhammad Ali . . ." then call him Clay throughout the article. This was *The New York Times* policy, for example; the editors refused to refer to him as Ali until he legally changed his name (although eventually they relented).

Ali's answer to the policy was "Why do I have to go to a white man's court to change a name given to a slave?"

Individual sportswriters, during interviews, often compromised by calling him "Champ." He would get angry at being called "Cassius," and many of the more arrogant, old-line journalists just couldn't get their mouths around "Muhammad."

Ali was optimistic it would turn out all right. "One good thing about America," he said, "you stand up for your rights and people will eventually adjust to it. Like my name."

His faith in America was just beginning to be tested.

14

Vietnam

On February 17, 1966, the air was sluggish and sweet in the Miami afternoon. Ali sat on a lawn chair under a palm tree outside his rented gray cement house, watching the neighborhood children straggle home from school. He called to them, and they bantered back and forth. He was relaxed and feeling good. He had run hard that morning, and just finished training in Dundee's gym. He was rounding into shape for his March fight against Ernie Terrell in Chicago. Someone shouted from inside the house, and he asked the children to excuse him. He had to take a long-distance phone call.

That morning, the Senate Foreign Relations Committee had conducted a televised hearing on the war in Vietnam. There had been a sharp exchange between Senator Wayne Morse of Oregon and General Maxwell D. Taylor on the conduct of the war and on home-front attitudes.

Senator Morse charged that General Taylor and President Johnson had misguided the public about the war. He was on the verge, it seemed, of calling them liars.

General Taylor implied that critics of the war, like the senator, were aiding the enemy. He was on the verge, it seemed, of calling the senator a traitor.

Although history would eventually prove the senator right, the general's opinion was more popular at the time. There was strong public feeling against anti-war "peaceniks."

Ali, until that day, had never really come out for or against the war. But people were beginning to wonder why someone in such good health wasn't in the Army.

Ali had originally been classified 1Y, which meant he wasn't quite up to Army mental standards and would only be drafted in an emergency. When politicians and veterans' groups questioned his classification, Ali was retested, and he still failed to come up to the 1A or "qualified" level.

Many people found it very hard to believe that Ali wasn't qualified. He was obviously in excellent physical condition, and despite his membership in an unpopular religious group there seemed nothing wrong with his psychological health. As for his intelligence, anyone who could create and recite so much poetry and give so many radio and television interviews had to be smart enough to remember his General Orders and spit shine his boots and fire a gun.

There had always been a dark rumor that the Louisville draft board had given Cassius Clay a deferment as a gift to the local millionaires who owned his contract. But now the last option on that contract was running out and Ali was set not only to own himself but to promote fights through a company he had organized with Herbert Muhammad and other Muslim leaders.

Thus it all seemed more than coincidental that on this mild Miami afternoon Ali should find out, by telephone call from a wire-service reporter, that he had just been reclassified 1A.

In his anger and bewilderment, he blurted, "Why me? I can't understand it. How did they do this to me—the heavyweight champion of the world?"

Soon, bright-red television trucks pulled up at the house. Interview followed interview on the lawn, while the children, unaware of the seriousness of the occasion, jostled to get into camera range.

"I've got a question," Ali shouted into the thicket of microphones. "For two years the government caused me international embarrassment, letting people think I was a nut. Sure it bothered me, and my mother and father suffered, and now they jump up and make me 1A without even an official notification or a test. Why did they let me be considered a nut, an illiterate, for two years?"

Several interviewers suggested that Ali might be called into the Army within several weeks. This was untrue; in fact, because of draft procedures, it was impossible, but they said it to goad Ali into wilder, more sensational quotes.

It worked.

"How can they do this without another test to see if I'm any wiser or worser than last time? Why are they so anxious, why are they gunning for me? All those thousands of young men are 1A in Louisville, and I don't think they need but thirty, and they have to go into two-year-old files to seek me out."

Between interviews he sat on the lawn chair, incongruously humming "Blowin' in the Wind," while Muslim bodyguards and friends kept whispering to him that it was all part of a white-devil plot. They offered stories of their own experiences with racial discrimination in the Army during World War II and the Korean War.

A Muslim predicted that Ali would never get through basic training alive: "Some fat cracker sergeant gonna blow you up on the hand-grenade range."

Ali was set off again.

"I'm fighting for the government every day. Why are they so anxious to pay me $80 a month when the government is in trouble financially?

"I think it costs them $12 million a day to stay in Vietnam. I buy a lot of bullets, at least three jet bombers a year, and pay the salary of 50,000 fighting men with the money they take from me after my fights."

Reporters kept asking Ali what he thought about the war in Vietnam, and he kept shrugging. He didn't know very much about the war. They couldn't believe it. News about the war, reports on battles and casualties, arguments about United States involvement in Southeast Asia, stories about draft dodgers and deserters and conscientious objectors, appeared in every telecast and in every edition of every newspaper.

Somehow the reporters couldn't understand that just because Ali was famous didn't mean he had to be well informed on foreign affairs. He was a poor reader, and mostly interested in news about himself on television.

Or maybe the reporters understood all this and were just digging and needling and pushing and prodding until they got a hot story. This was 1966, and the country as a whole had not yet decided the war was a terrible, immoral mistake: Talking *against* the war, as mostly students and professors were doing, was very unpopular and sometimes dangerous. The reporters kept asking their questions, Do you know why we are fighting in Vietnam? and Where is Vietnam? and What do you think about the Vietcong? Ali kept shrugging out of ignorance.

Tired, exasperated, angry at being made to feel stupid by his interviewers, feeling betrayed by his government, he finally blurted, "I ain't got nothing against them Vietcong."

15

On the Road

"I ain't got nothing against them Vietcong."

Years later, after the March on the Pentagon and the Pentagon Papers, after the Moratorium and the shootings at Kent State, after the suicides and the murders and the beatings and the persecution and the lies and the terrible troubles that beset America because of its wrongful involvement in a faraway war, those words by a boxer don't seem so wild or dangerous.

But in 1966, when most Americans still thought their country's participation was righteous and noble, even necessary to national security, those words marked Muhammad Ali as a traitor in many people's minds.

State governments and boxing commissions and veterans' groups and editorial writers waved that quote like a bloody flag. They used it to drive Ali out of the country. They said they were afraid that Ali, if allowed to remain an athletic hero in America, would encourage other young people to turn their backs on their patriotic duty.

The Chicago bout against Terrell was canceled. No other American city would sanction the match. A movement was begun to take away Ali's heavyweight title. The World Boxing Association, a loose federation of state and city boxing commissions, stepped up its efforts to have Ernie Terrell declared the true champion without ever having to step in the ring with Ali. Boxing promotors, who generally ignored the W.B.A. —in fact laughed at the group—now saw it as a way of knocking out Ali.

Ali's first four fights in 1966 were outside the U.S. He was an unusually active champion, defending the title against all comers. The first foreign fight was in Toronto against George Chuvalo, the tough Canadian champion. Ali had trouble keeping his mind on boxing matters.

"All great men have to suffer," he told me in Toronto one day. "Jesus was condemned, Moses, Noah, Elijah, Martin Luther King. To be great, you suffer, you have to pay the price. Why are so many powers on me?

"A big Negro movie star called me up. He said, 'You're showing us that we're not free either.' Another big Negro calls up. 'You're doing something we don't have the courage to do.'

"I'm run out of my own country, it makes me bigger. I always knew I was meant for something. It's taking shape, a divine destiny."

There were many foreign reporters in Toronto, and unlike their American counterparts they tended to treat Ali as a visiting dignitary instead of as a news source to be skeptically interviewed. They were charmed by his patience with their questions and by his accessibility, but they also enjoyed the opportunity of using him to attack the American involvement in Vietnam.

"The Americans are envious," a Dutchman told Ali, "because you speak the truth."

"Let other people defend me," replied Ali with a grand wave, "because to defend myself would be cheapening."

"You are beloved in my country," said a Turk. "On the streets of Istanbul children wear pictures of you on their shirts and cry, 'I am the Greatest.' "

"They do, really?" asked Ali, delighted. "Then tell your people that I will visit Turkey right after I beat Chuvalo."

He beat Chuvalo, but he didn't go to Turkey. He went to England, for fights with Henry Cooper and Brian London, and to Germany, for a fight with Karl Mildenberger. He won them all easily. He also ended his relationship with the Louisville Sponsoring Group; the six years of the contract were over.

Traveling was very broadening for Ali. Because he was a symbol of American dissent to many foreigners, he attracted intellectuals and students and political leaders instead of just boxing fans. He was flattered by this new attention, and he began to think and speak in more worldly terms. "Elijah is not teaching hate when he tells us about all the evil things that the white man done, any more than you're teaching hate when you tell about what Hitler did to the Jews. That's not hate, that's history."

To the African and Indian students who sought him out, he explained that those who were against him "don't like me because I'm free. The Negro has always sold himself out for money or women, but I give up everything for what I believe. I'm a free man, I don't belong to anybody."

By leaving America, Ali became better known to Americans. His fights were usually replayed on the ABC television network, and more people saw him fight on their home sets than on the previous closed-circuit telecasts. They also heard him speak—usually in interviews with Howard Cosell, whose defense of Ali, on constitutional grounds, was one of the bravest and most important pieces of sports journalism in the Sixties.

By late 1966, the forces that had kept Ali from fighting in the United States relented. Perhaps they felt he was gaining too positive an image abroad, perhaps they didn't want to risk his staying in Europe to avoid the draft. In any case, the door was reopened and he fought and won three more times—for his own Muslim-sponsored company—before the door was slammed shut again.

Against Cleveland Williams he unveiled the "Ali Shuffle," a meaningless soft-shoe dance he used to break the monotony of a mismatch.

Against tall Ernie Terrell he unleashed a "chastise-ment" similar to the one he had used on Floyd Patterson. As had Floyd, Ernie insisted upon calling him Clay instead of Ali, and the champion battered him unmercifully while shouting, "What's my name, Uncle Tom? . . . Give me another Clay, you white man's nigger. . . ."

The outburst helped convince *The Ring* magazine not to select its usual Fighter of the Year. Ali was obviously the best fighter around, but *The Ring* declared that "most emphatically is Cassius Clay of Louisville not to be held up as an example to the youngsters of America."

Terrell, his vision still blurry from the beating, thought *The Ring* was wrong. He declared: "It's illegitimate reasoning and it's out of the realm of *The Ring*. This will be used as a stepping-stone for the Muslims to say they achieved something. If Clay did something illegal, put him in jail. But he didn't. I dislike what Clay stands for, using boxing to further an extremist cause. But it's not against the law to be a clown."

Ali gained allies among black leaders. Dr. Martin Luther King, Jr., was joined by Congressman Adam Clayton Powell and Georgia legislator Julian Bond in citing Ali as an example of black manhood standing tall against an illegal and immoral system.

By the spring of 1967, Ali had made it very clear he would not serve in the armed forces. His lawyers were trying to secure him a deferment either as a conscientious objector—a person morally opposed to war—or as a Minister of Islam. Clergymen were automatically exempted from duty if they so chose. Muslims as a rule did not go into the Army; during World War II Elijah himself had been jailed for draft evasion.

The day before the Terrell fight at the Houston Astrodome, half a dozen white reporters and photographers were invited to hear Ali preach at the local Muslim mosque. We all figured it was part of a publicity stunt to substantiate Ali's claim to deferment as a minister, but it was too good a story to pass up on any grounds.

We were thoroughly searched at the door, as was the custom with all outsiders, black or white, and our ball-point pens were clicked in our faces in case they contained tiny hidden weapons.

Ali, relaxed and well rehearsed, told the crowd, which contained many curious non-Muslim blacks, that while heredity and talent had made him strong and a good fighter, "the teachings of Elijah made me heavyweight champion."

He then launched into a disgusting, stomach-turning lecture on the evils of eating pork. He made snuffling pig noises and he drew sketches on the blackboard of what he called "the nastiest animal in the world—the swine—a mouthful of maggots and pus. They bred the cat and the rat and the dog and came up with the hog." He told the audience that one of the reasons Negroes didn't get ahead was because years of eating ham and bacon and pigs feet and chitterlings and pork chops had ruined their minds and their bodies. The Muslims were very strict at that time in their dietary laws, which were similar to the kosher rules of Orthodox Jews.

After about fifteen minutes of the pork lecture, we whites were asked to leave the mosque. Ali spoke for another hour, according to a black reporter who stayed. He told how the "blue-eyed white devils" were created in a laboratory by an evil black scientist (according to Muslim mythology, the original people on earth were black). Someday, all the whites would be destroyed by skinny, seven-foot men "who never smile," warriors of Allah who circle the earth on space platforms.

In cold print, it all seems no more or less nutty than some other religious tales, but it had a powerful effect on blacks in those days who had never before heard black preachers put down whites in such tough and graphic words.

Ali's last fight before his long "exile" was held in the old Madison Square Garden between 49th and 50th Streets in New York, that famous arena irreverently known as "The Mecca of Boxing."

It was the first time Ali had ever fought there as champion. Ironically, just a few weeks after he had originally won the title in 1964, Garden officials had refused to introduce him from the ring with other guests one night if he insisted upon being introduced as Muhammad Ali instead of Cassius Clay.

Rather than be introduced as Cassius Clay, the champion kept his seat. It was a gross breach of boxing etiquette on the Garden's part—not introducing the heavyweight champ at a prizefight is like refusing to acknowledge that the President of the United States is visiting the Senate.

But a scant two years later, Garden officials put the name Muhammad Ali on the marquee. This time, obviously, there was money to be made. And they promoted the fight, against an aging boxer named Zora Folley, as "the last chance to see Ali before he gets one to three," a reference to the then-current sentence for refusal to be drafted.

There was little else to recommend the match. Folley was a nice man who called the champ "Mr. Ali" and seemed more interested in getting autographs for his eight children than in hitting him. In the seventh round, after giving Folley a respectable run for his good behavior, Ali knocked him out with the same short right that had decked Liston. It was the last Ali punch the public would see for more than three years.

"When I'm gone," Ali predicted, "boxing be nothing again. The fans with the cigars and the hats turned down will be there, but no more housewives and little men in the street and foreign presidents. It's going to be back to the fighter who comes to town, smells a flower, visits a hospital, blows a horn, and says he's in shape. Old hat.

"I was the onliest boxer in history people asked questions like a senator."

16

In Exile

Two days before he was scheduled to be drafted into the Army, Muhammad Ali sat in a Chicago motel coffee shop and watched Lake Michigan roll beneath an April storm. His own mood was dark and unsettled, too. His deferment had not come through, but he was determined not to go into the Army.

"I don't want to go to jail," he said, "but I've got to live the life my conscience and my God tell me to. What does it profit me to be the wellest-liked man in America who sold out everybody?"

Someone at his table asked, "Why don't you skip the country?"

He looked horrified. "You serious? I got to stay here and lead my people to the right man, Elijah Muhammad."

I reminded him that many people felt his life would

be in danger whether he went into the Army or to jail.

"Every day they die in Vietnam for nothing," he said. "I might as well die right here for something."

A reporter asked, "What about just playing the game like other big-time athletes? You wouldn't be sent to the front lines. You could give exhibitions and teach physical fitness."

Ali leaned across the table, his eyes suddenly bright, and he spoke with absolute conviction. "What can you give me, America, for turning down my religion? You want me to do what the white man says and go fight a war against some people I don't know nothing about, get some freedom for some other people when my own people can't get theirs here?

"You want me to be so scared of the white man I'll go and get two arms shot off and ten medals so you can give me a small salary and pat my head and say, 'Good boy, he fought for his country'?"

Breakfast stretched into lunch on that gray, damp morning in Chicago. Others came to the table, some stayed, some only stopped to shake his hand and wish him luck. Most of the visitors were white men, and they seemed genuinely moved by his determination to stand his ground. There was no question that he was prepared to go to prison.

Yet even as Ali moved inexorably toward his darkest time, there were indications that the mood of the country was shifting in his favor. People who had no sympathy for his beliefs were impressed by his willingness to sacrifice for those beliefs. People were just beginning to realize that he was sincere, that he was ready to give up his money, his career, his freedom, for what he believed was right.

Sitting in that motel coffee shop that day he slowly began to respond to the undercurrent of support. His mood lightened, his eyes softened, his voice deepened and dropped.

"Ah-lee will return," he intoned. "My ghost will haunt all arenas. The people will watch the fights and they will whisper, 'Hey, Ali could whip that guy. . . . You think so? . . . Sure. . . . No, he couldn't. . . . Wish he'd come out of retirement. . . .'

"Twenty-five years old now. Make my comeback at twenty-eight. That's not old. Whip 'em all—if I get good food in jail."

A newcomer to the table said it was all so very sad that such a handsome and gifted young man should have to even contemplate death and imprisonment. Ali straightened, his eyes bright again, perhaps like martyrs' eyes reflecting the licking flames.

"Allah okays the adversary to try us. That's how He sees if you're a true believer.

"All a man has got to show for his time here on earth is what kind of a name he had. Jesus. Columbus. Daniel Boone. Now, take Wyatt Earp. . . . Who would have told him when he was fighting crooks and standing up for principles that there'd be a television show about him? That kids on the street would say, 'I'm Wyatt Earp. *Reach.*' "

He recited a new poem:

Two thousand years from now,
Muhammad Ali, Muhammad Ali,
He roamed the Western Hemisphere,
He was courageous and strong,
He called the round when the clown hit the ground.
Tell little children whatever they believe,
Stand up like Muhammad Ali.

Two days later, on April 28, 1967, in Houston, Texas, Ali refused to take the symbolic one step forward during Army induction ceremonies that would have signified his willingness to be drafted. He stood absolutely still when his name was called. Instead of becoming Private Cassius Clay, he became a Federal case.

In one sense, the non-step was a non-event. He was not arrested on the spot and there were no great public demonstrations for or against him. He had top lawyers, money, and fame—he could be sure that his case would not be swept under the rug. Many young American men without lawyers or money or fame, but with strong moral convictions, simply went to jail for refusing to be drafted, and stayed behind bars for as long as five years.

But, in another sense, Ali's non-step was a turning point in his public life. He was confirming himself, he was authenticating his credo, "I don't have to be what you want me to be. I'm free to be who I want."

Other athletes, even those who regarded him as a loudmouth and a clown, were appalled at the speed by which boxing commissions throughout the country withdrew their recognition of Ali as champion, usually on grounds of "conduct detrimental to boxing."

Black athletes without Muslim sympathies were disturbed that a man could be stripped of his livelihood without due process of law. He had not been convicted of any crime. In fact, the boxing commissions acted before he had even been *charged* with a crime.

First athletes, then fans, then people outside sports began to regard the case of *United States of America* v. *Cassius Marcellus Clay, Jr., also known as Muhammad Ali* as an example of the system crushing the right of an individual to dissent.

And what an individual! The heavyweight champ of the world.

Some people thought, Wow, if this can happen to the champ, think what the system could do to little old me, and they kept their mouths shut and tucked in their heads.

Other people thought, Hey, this is a warning, we better stand up for our rights now, or we just won't have any.

Because sports touches people of every age group, economic class, and political leaning, the Ali case had enormous ramifications. Ali's politics were certainly not left wing, but passionate young radicals regarded him as a hero. And even traditionally conservative baseball and football players, particularly blacks, were inspired in their own growing militancy against what they regarded as oppression by professional club owners, team managers, college coaches, and the officials of amateur sports.

Although Ali made several appearances at civil rights meetings and peace demonstrations, most notably for the Congress of Racial Equality and for Dr. King, he did not become involved in the growing antiwar, antiadministration movements. Such actions would have been frowned on by Elijah. The Muslims refused to participate in "white man's politics" in those days. Also, Ali's lawyers had advised him to keep a low profile while his case dragged on. Ali made it plain that he had no intention of becoming "a Negro leader."

In the summer of 1967 he married Belinda Boyd, a seventeen-year-old Muslim, and he slipped off the front pages.

The three and a half years of his "exile," as Ali refers to his forced retirement from boxing, may have been the most intellectually enriching of his life. For the first time since he was twelve years old, his mind and body were freed from the demands of serious training. It was a time of intense education. Although the government would not allow him to leave the country, he traveled extensively within America—for court appearances, Muslim meetings, and campus speeches. He became one of the most popular speakers on the college lecture circuit, often earning two or three thousand dollars for a single speech he might repeat four or five times a week.

The college engagements not only honed his speaking style, but broadened his awareness of current events; students often challenged his diatribes against marijuana and "mixed" racial dating, and although he didn't change his position he was forced to explain them on a more rational and less religious level. He was also forced to think them through for himself.

He practiced his speechmaking with the same zeal he had brought to boxing, writing and rewriting the speeches on giant white index cards, reading them to Belinda, reading them in front of a full-length mirror, reading them into a tape recorder, then listening to the playback and criticizing himself. Gradually, as his self-confidence grew and his religious references became more assured, he lost his early stiffness and became a smooth and relaxed speaker.

But his college audiences suffered through the sometimes boring speeches on inspirational and religious themes (titles included "The Intoxication of Fame" and "Friendship and Self-Interest") for the lively question-and-answer sessions afterward, in which he'd talk about boxing and offer such Ali-isms as "I ain't the Greatest no more because Allah is the Greatest. But I'm still the prettiest."

He said he gave up being the prettiest on June 18, 1968, when Maryum was born. She was the first of the four children he had with Belinda, who by now had taken the Muslim name Khalilah.

In 1969 Ali appeared in a Broadway musical, *Buck White*. It was not a very good show, and it didn't last too long, but his singing voice was adequate to the role, and the stage experience was valuable. His contract with the producers was one of the most unusual in show business: The contract was to terminate ten days before any scheduled jail term began, and Ali was to have the right to delete any words or phrases he considered objectionable. Since the musical was about various black ghetto characters plotting a poverty-program swindle, it depended for its flavor and comedy on four-letter words, "slanguage," and sexual and racial jokes. By the time Ali finished deleting, there wasn't much soul left in the show.

Around that time he also began working on his autobiography with Richard Durham, which forced him to think through and reevaluate many aspects of his life. The result, *The Greatest*, was a disappointment to readers who expected Ali to make a serious effort to explain his life truthfully. Ali apparently agreed to do the book only because he needed the money, not out of any burning need to counteract a decade of sportswriter disinformation.

Also for money, he became involved in a fast-food hamburger chain called "Champburger," which never got off the ground, and a movie dramatization of a hypothetical boxing match between him and Rocky Marciano, a former champion. After being cut to ribbons by Ali's quick fists, Marciano, drenched in stage blood, "knocked out" Ali in the thirteenth round. According to the film's producer, the ending had been "written" by a computer which had swallowed all the information on the two fighters and spat up a Marciano victory.

Despite his hustling, money was sometimes short, and some friends drifted away. He was out of the spotlight he loved. There was a new champion now, Joe Frazier. Ali tried to stay in shape, to run every day and occasionally spar, but it was hard to train without the deadline of a scheduled fight. Ali didn't know if he would ever be allowed to fight again. And even if he was, every passing day made it harder and harder for him to regain his rusting skills.

His legal battles dragged on. He had finally been convicted of draft evasion, and a judge had thrown the book at him—five years in jail and a $10,000 fine. Ali's lawyers were keeping him out of jail by bringing up technicalities and filing appeals. (As it turned out, the only time Ali ever spent in jail as a prisoner had nothing to do with his draft case—in December 1968 he spent eight days in a Miami jail on an old speeding conviction he had neglected to attend to. The original sentence was 10 days, but he was released early, with other prisoners, in a Christmas amnesty.)

For one year of his exile he was suspended from the Muslims. The precise reason is still not clear, but Muslims have said that it had to do with his show-business activities and with his continued efforts to get a license to fight. Elijah interpreted these actions, it was said, as a sign that Ali had temporarily forsaken Allah and was trying to solve his own problems, an expression of loss of faith.

There were small humiliations that underscored his fall from the throne. He appeared on the TV show *What's My Line?* as mystery guest. The blindfolded panelists were unable to guess his identity by asking yes-or-no questions. Five years earlier, on the same show, the panelists had guessed his identity in seconds. He just wasn't a household name in 1969.

When he returned to the New York Hilton after the taping of the show, he found that his key no longer opened the lock on his door. The hotel had locked him out of his own room. An assistant manager explained that Ali's credit rating was so poor he would have to pay his bill—in cash—before they would let him back in.

His bill was only $53.09.

After he paid, the assistant manager and the hotel detective asked him for his autograph. He was very patient and courteous and he signed their slips of paper. I was with him that day, and I was far more outraged than he was. He shrugged it off. When you're the champ, he said, they never make you pay right away. It's only when you're down and busted they want their money up front. That's the way of the world.

If Ali's spirit sometimes flagged, he kept up a brave front. But there were times he seemed on a treadmill to oblivion, driving aimlessly around Chicago, where he now lived, visiting neighborhood barbershops to gossip, dropping in on Muslim restaurants to fill up on navy-bean pie, hanging out in Herbert Muhammad's office at the Muslim newspaper, *Muhammad Speaks*, creating little chores to get himself out of the house. He began to get fat.

Meanwhile, the nation that had turned away from him was turning back. Irwin Shaw, the novelist, headed a group of writers and editors demanding his reinstatement. The students and teachers he had met on the college circuit formed another group clamoring for fair play, especially after it was discovered that the FBI had illegally gathered evidence against him through wiretaps on the phones of Elijah and Dr. King.

In the light of new information about the conduct of the Vietnam War, his remarks no longer seemed so treacherous and inflammatory. His Muslim affiliation was no longer considered so dangerous to the national security; far from the revolutionaries they had been described as, the Muslims turned out to be hardworking believers in black capitalism.

To non-Muslim blacks, Ali became more and more a symbol of black manhood; one year he was asked to be Grand Marshal of the annual Watts Parade in Los Angeles. Meanwhile, his closest white business associates, the lawyer Robert Arum and the promotor-publicist Harold Conrad, never gave up the search for a state or city boxing commission that would license him to fight.

The Supreme Court began reviewing his conviction. In the light of the Court's 1970 Welsh decision, in which moral and ethical objection to war was judged as legally valid as formal religious objection, it looked as though the high court would have to overturn his conviction, whether or not it judged him to be a true minister of the faith.

At the same time, civil liberties lawyers in New York had prepared an impressive list of convicted murderers, burglars, and armed robbers who had been licensed to fight by the New York State Athletic Commission; obviously, the Commission's ruling—that

Ali's conduct in refusing to be drafted was detrimental to the sport—would not stand up to a serious judicial challenge.

But it was black power that brought Ali back to the ring. Black political power. A black Georgia state senator, Leroy Johnson, swinging his voting bloc like a war club, engineered the licensing of a match between Ali and Jerry Quarry, a respected white contender, in Atlanta. The city's liberal white mayor, Sam Massell, called the fight a "demonstration in democracy." Such national black figures as Andrew Young, Jesse Jackson, Julian Bond, Ralph Abernathy, Coretta Scott King, Sidney Poitier, Bill Cosby, Diana Ross, and Henry Aaron lent their prestige and glitter to the event.

Ali did not let them down. On October 26, 1970, moving with silken speed and hitting hard, Ali knocked out Quarry in the third round. The three-and-a-half-year exile was over.

After the fight, Mrs. King called Ali a "champion of justice and peace and unity."

Dr. Abernathy, presenting Ali with the annual Dr. King award, called him "the March on Washington all in two fists."

17

THE FIGHT

Ali was back, but was he still the king?

Joe Frazier, a twenty-seven-year-old sharecropper's son from Beaufort, South Carolina, said NO! But Smokin' Joe, who had taken over the heavyweight crown during Ali's exile, knew he would be considered a pretender until he actually beat Ali in the ring. It didn't matter that Frazier had beaten every other ranking heavyweight, that he had knocked out most of them, that he had never been beaten in his professional career. Nothing really counted until he beat Ali.

Their meeting, on March 8, 1971, was advertised, quite simply, as THE FIGHT. The two best heavyweight boxers of their time, both Olympic gold-medal winners, both undefeated as professionals, both claimants to the same throne. The place was the new Madison Square Garden on 33d Street in New York. The purse was an unprecedented $2.5 million *each*, win, lose, or draw.

Ali was larger than Frazier, four inches taller at six feet three inches, ten pounds heavier at 215, and his arms were several inches longer, an important statistic for a fighter who wants to hit without getting hit.

But Ali, at 29, was two years older than Frazier and he had been out of condition and out of practice for three and a half years in the prime of his boxing life, while Frazier had fought and improved his skills.

For many people, THE FIGHT was more than just a fight. It was a morality play; some saw it as the prince returning from exile, the most charismatic and controversial hero in the history of sport against the squat, powerful, awesome punching machine who stood between him and his rightful place; others saw it as the final chapter in the public life of an evil con man who would be reduced to his hollow self by a rough, brawling farmer representing honest Americanism.

Whatever THE FIGHT was, it was obviously more than a sporting event. It was a moment in history.

But it was also a terrific fight. It lasted fifteen of the most grueling, brutal rounds the celebrity-studded crowd had ever seen.

They had expected Smokin' Joe to come out "smoking," slugging, bulling Ali around the ring, smashing at Ali's body. They had expected Joe to plant his feet and pound away, offering up his own bumpy face in sacrifice to eventual victory. Joe didn't disappoint them.

But Ali's strategy was a shock. They expected the dancing master to jab and run, to spin and turn and skip around the ring, to make Frazier chase him.

But Ali did not run that night. He stood and he fought.

With the same self-confidence, the same willfulness, the same arrogance that had made him a champion, that had given him the strength to defy the American government, he tried to create a masterpiece.

It wasn't enough for him to beat Joe Frazier—he was determined to prove he could take Frazier's best shots, that he could outslug the slugger. He saw the fight as the proving of his manhood.

His basic strategy was to stand against the ropes and let Frazier bang against his arms and shoulders, hoping Frazier would burn himself out. But Ali underestimated Frazier's strength and conditioning, and overestimated his own. In the last round, his *hubris*, what the ancient Greek playwrights called overweening pride, was dramatically exposed. Frazier knocked him down. Ali got up, but it didn't matter. The official scorecards were unanimous in the decision for Frazier, and the crowd applauded their judgment.

The physical toll of THE FIGHT was visible. Frazier's face, misshapen and skinned, looked unfamiliar afterward. He was later hospitalized for internal injuries. For the first time in Ali's career, he looked as though he had truly been in a fight. His face was lumpy and blotched, his body marked and sore.

Yet both men came out winners. Frazier was no

longer under Ali's shadow: He was undisputed champion of the world, and he was respected as a superb fighter.

Ali had proven something, too. No one had ever doubted his speed or his talent, but his courage in the ring, his "heart," as boxing fans called it, had always been suspect. Now there was no doubt that Ali had heart, that he could take it, and that he had, indeed, come back.

The day after the fight, Ali was as cool and self-assured in defeat as he had always been in victory.

"Just lost a fight, that's all. More important things to worry about in life," he said. "Probably be a better man for it."

Journalists in his hotel suite that day tried to make him comment on the importance of his defeat, but Ali would have none of it.

"News don't last too long," said Ali. "Plane crash, ninety people die, it's not news no more a day after. My losing not so important as ninety people dying. Presidents get assassinated, civil rights leaders get assassinated, you don't hear so much about that no more.

"The world goes on, you got children to feed and bills to pay, got other things to worry about. You all be writing about something else soon. I had my day. You lose, you lose. You don't shoot yourself."

He stirred in the chair from which he had been receiving guests all morning. "A great leader has his followers. When the leader fails, his followers cry. I don't cry, so maybe they won't cry. I have to rejoice in defeat like I rejoiced in victory so my followers can conquer their defeats, the tragedies every day. Someone in the family dies, you lose your property . . ."

A radio reporter interrupted him. "Champ . . ."

"Don't call me the champ," said Ali gently. "Joe's the champ now."

I said to him, "Muhammad, remember before the first Liston fight when you said that if you lost you'd be on the street the next day hollering 'No man ever beat me twice'?"

A smile spread slowly across Ali's scuffed face. "I remember. And you know what I say now? Get me Joe Frazier. . . . No man ever beat me twice. . . ."

His voice rose, his words tumbled out.

". . . I'll get by Joe this time. . . . I'll straighten this out. . . . I'm ready this time. . . . Joe, you hear me. . . .

"JOE, IF YOU BEAT ME THIS TIME YOU'LL REALLY BE THE GREATEST."

18

Case Closed

At nine-fifteen on the morning of June 28, 1971, Muhammad Ali was tooling around the South Side of Chicago in his green-and-white Lincoln Mark III when he was suddenly struck by a powerful thirst for fresh-squeezed orange juice. He whipped the big car around a corner and came to a screeching stop in front of an orange juice stand. As he stepped out of the car, a man came running toward him shouting, "I just heard it on the radio. The Supreme Court said you're free."

Ali whooped, said, "Thanks to Allah," and dived back into his car to turn on his own radio. It was true. The Court had decided that Ali *should not have been drafted in the first place.*

Furthermore, the Court accused the Justice Department of misleading draft authorities by falsely advising them that Ali's claim as a conscientious objector was neither sincere nor based on religious tenets.

Case closed. The years of uncertainty were over.

Ali jumped out of his car and ordered a round of orange juice for everyone within shouting distance.

"This case proves," said one of Ali's lawyers, Robert Arum, "that our justice system works—if you have the money and the influence to go all the way."

Later that day, at a press conference, Ali was asked if he would sue those who had prevented him from earning his living as a boxer during the years of his exile.

"No," he answered. "They only did what they thought was right at the time. I did what I thought was right. That was all. I can't condemn them for doing what they think was right."

19

The Rumble in the Jungle

Joe Frazier held his undisputed title for less than two years. He lost it to a powerhouse slugger named George Foreman, also an Olympic champion. If there had been any hope that Ali would someday win back the title, it seemed gone now. Foreman was as big as Ali, more heavily muscled, a water buffalo in the ring.

Ali kept fighting after he lost to Frazier—in fact he fought fourteen times in the next three years, an unusually active schedule. He fought every heavyweight contender available, from his old sparring partner and boyhood friend, Jimmy Ellis, to his old enemy, Floyd Patterson. He fought and whipped Jerry Quarry again. He beat the tall, lean, light-heavyweight champion, Bob Foster, but suffered his very first cut, a slash over his left eye that required five stitches to close. He lost to a rising young fighter, Ken Norton, who broke his jaw. He beat Norton in a rematch, then beat Joe Frazier in their rematch.

He never fought for less than $200,000 a bout, and sometimes for twice as much, or more. His total ring earnings for those fourteen fights were more than $5 million, an incredible sum for a man who wasn't even the champion.

As incredible as that sum was for fourteen fights, Ali would make as much for just one: the fight on October 30, 1974, in Kinshasa, Zaire, against George Foreman, for the heavyweight title of the world. The fight that Ali, with characteristic whimsy, called "The Rumble in the Jungle."

Each fighter was guaranteed $5 million, the fattest purse in history. The site was historical, too. Zaire had once been the Belgian Congo, known for rape and murder and massacre. Now, free of European rule, it was intensely nationalistic under President Mobutu Sese Seko, who had ordered roadside signs that read:

A FIGHT BETWEEN TWO BLACKS IN A BLACK NATION ORGANIZED BY BLACKS AND SEEN BY THE WHOLE WORLD; THIS IS THE VICTORY OF MOBUTISM.

THE COUNTRY OF ZAIRE WHICH HAS BEEN BLED BECAUSE OF PILLAGE AND SYSTEMATIC EXPLOITATION MUST BECOME A FORTRESS AGAINST IMPERIALISM AND A SPEARHEAD FOR THE LIBERATION OF THE AFRICAN CONTINENT.

Ali seemed to revel in the African setting. He re-
peated Bundini's aphorism, "The world is a black shirt
with a few white buttons," and he talked about the
strength that flowed into his body from the earth of his
"ancestral home."

He could also poke fun at all the publicity and
hyperbole. He sat one morning on a lawn that curved
down to the Congo River and told Peter Bonventre of
Newsweek: "This is just another boxing match between a colored boy from Kentucky and a colored boy
from Houston. Nothing to get excited about, or scared.
I've had appointments with danger, sneered at doom,
chuckled in the face of catastrophe, stood fearless in
the hour of horror. An occasion like this is fitted to
me."

(While it was a characteristic Ali declamation, it
was also very much like a speech Paul Robeson made
in his 1933 film *The Emperor Jones.*)

And so, in the dark stillness of the hour before
dawn, beneath a waning African moon, George Foreman, the favorite to win, shrugged his cannonball
shoulders and stared balefully at Ali. Foreman, who
was twenty-five years old, had never even been
knocked off his feet in a prizefight. Ali, now thirty-two,
considered to be in the twilight of his career, could no
longer even depend on his greatest gift—his once-daz-
zling speed.

But Ali, without fear, smiled at Foreman and softly said: "You have heard of me since you were young. You've been following me since you were a little boy. Now you must meet me, your master!"

Millions were watching on closed-circuit television around the world. In the stadium at Kinshasa, thousands began to chant "Ali, bomayé"—Kill him, Ali.

As Ali waited for the opening round, the voice of Bundini, who had been with him when he beat Sonny Liston, cut through the swelling roar of the crowd: "Remember what I said. God set it up this way. This is the closing of the book. The king gained his throne by killing a monster, and the king will regain his throne by killing a bigger monster. This is the closing of the book."

At the bell, the two big men charged to the center of the ring. They stopped, circled each other warily for a moment. Then Ali delivered the first punch, a powerful right to Foreman's head. Foreman lunged forward in rage, and Ali grabbed him around the neck and pushed his head down. No one had ever hit Big George so hard and so early, and no one before had ever dared to test his strength by grappling with him.

A few minutes later, Foreman drove Ali into the ropes and began to pummel him. The crowd groaned. Ali was trapped! But Ali frustrated Foreman's attack by letting the best of his blows bounce off his arms and shoulders.

Boxing experts at ringside buzzed with consternation. They had never seen such an Ali. He was not dancing, he was merely bobbing from side to side. He was throwing rights—a dangerous tactic against a slugger like Foreman because it left him open to counterattack. He had always saved his right for later in a fight, when he had worn down his opponent. And he was letting Foreman push him against the ropes and slug, obviously trying to drain Foreman's punching strength. But Ali was seven years older than Foreman, and it seemed unlikely that such a tactic could work, that he could survive this pace for very long.

So much for experts. Except for a moment in the second round when Ali seemed momentarily rocked by a hard shot to his head, he was the master indeed.

Characteristically, his approach was unorthodox and filled with jeopardy. His arms and shoulders were absorbing Foreman's thundering punches, but the spring of the ring ropes he was leaning on helped cushion the force of the blows.

And Foreman, a mechanical fighter who had been prepared to cuff away at a dancer and blast away at a target trying to push out of a trap, found himself poking straight ahead at an object that had no intention of trying to escape.

Ali punched right back, faster than Foreman, and he taunted him through his mouthpiece: "You are just an amateur, George. Show me something. Hit me hard."

By the fifth round, Foreman's face was lumped and his legs were heavy and slow. The pace was telling on him, not on the old man.

Foreman made a decision: He would have to go all

104

out now, throw everything he had and try to knock Ali out.

And Foreman threw it all, crunching rights and wicked left hooks, bombarding Ali's face and body. Foreman's chest seemed to be bursting with the effort of throwing a hundred punches, his very best.

And Ali still stood.

The crowd was on its feet roaring, "Ali, bomayé."

Foreman's punches began to grow weaker, and then he paused.

Now Ali's hands began to blur, a dozen thunderbolts, perhaps his hardest punches, a right cross that nearly turned Foreman's head around.

The end came, quite suddenly, in the eighth round. Some thought it was the finest, the hardest punch Ali had ever thrown, a punch he had saved since he was twelve years old for this glorious moment in his racial homeland.

First, he fired three good rights and a left. Then the Bomb, a right-hand sledgehammer. Foreman leaned forward from the waist, then pitched to the canvas.

Ali had killed the monster. He had closed the book. He had regained his throne. He was heavyweight champion of the world again.

He fainted. He was back on his feet in less than ten seconds, before most in the stadium were aware of what had happened.

He walked to the ring apron and looked down at the press. They had long since stopped expecting from him the traditional humility of the victorious athlete.

"What did I tell you?" he shouted. "I did it. I said I'd do it, but did you listen?"

This time, America celebrated his ascendency to the heavyweight throne. The mayors of Chicago and of New York welcomed him with ceremonies and poems and keys to their cities. There was a parade through Louisville. And President Ford received him in the Oval Office of the White House.

Ali said, "You made a big mistake letting me come, because now I'm going after your job."

20

The Once
and Future Champ

"People listen to me because I'm champ of the world," Ali was fond of saying. "That's why I keep fighting, so I can keep doing Allah's work. I'm on a divine mission. I was born to do what I'm doing. I'll be told when to retire."

And yet, watching him entertain the crowds that swarmed into his training sessions, his exhibitions, his public appearances, it was hard to believe that he fought only to maintain a platform from which to preach. He so obviously enjoyed being the champion, being the hero, being in the spotlight.

"The championship," he said one night in a mellow mood, "that's top of the world."

And it seemed even sweeter the second time around. There was much now of the old Cassius Clay, staging little surprise parties for the world with himself as guest of honor and gift.

Nothing seemed to delight him more than to suddenly appear—on a downtown street, in a residential neighborhood (black or white), in stores, arenas, restaurants, hotel lobbies, airport terminals—and watch people stop . . .

. . . turn . . .

. . . double-take . . .

. . . whisper, "Is that really . . . ?" and then, convinced by his open smile that it really was, stampede toward him crying, "Ah-leeeeeeeeee."

He was always more accessible than most celebrities, rarely turning down a request for an autograph or a handshake, even while eating, and as ready to make a speech or a poem for one little old lady as for millions on network television.

And his alertness was phenomenal; in their flustered haste, amateur photographers always seemed to forget to take off their lens caps or properly mount their flash cubes, and Ali was always quick to point it out lest their moment of glory with him go unrecorded.

He loved to kiss babies. Hug them, rub noses with them, cuddle them. "You remember this your whole life, your mommy and daddy remind you if you forget, and show you the picture. You was kissed by the champ."

And he would carefully explain: "One time Joe Louis came to Louisville and he leaned against a telephone pole on my street. Didn't mean nothing to him, how many poles you think he leaned on? But my momma never forgot. She still can't pass that telephone pole without telling us Joe Louis leaned on it. Nothing to him, big thing to her."

Or: "You never know what you're gonna get back when you invest in children. Might even grow up to be a lawyer. Defend you. It happens."

He often seemed as boyish and brimming as the old "Louisville Lip" himself, and he could take a joke now, even if it concerned his religion.

Once, during a flight, I noticed that his safety belt wasn't buckled. When I pointed it out, Ali said, "Don't need to."

"Why?"

"Nothing happen to me."

"How come?"

"I'm under divine protection."

"In that case," I said, "would you mind if I unbuckle my belt, too, and just hold your hand till we get back down again?"

Ali laughed, and he was still smiling when the stewardess brought us coffee. He wrinkled his nose as I drank mine black.

"How can you drink it like that?" he said.

"Black is pure and strong," I said, echoing one of Ali's old lines.

Ali poured lightener into his own cup, and mimicked me. "See, I'm integratin'."

But the new champion, happier, more relaxed, surer of his status in the world, was still the old champion who had said, "I don't have to be what you want me to be. I'm free to be who I want."

He was still never quite what people expected him to be, he fit no mold, he was, as Angelo Dundee often said, a man whom "you can't figure out. There's just no pattern to him. If you try to think what he's gonna do next, you're dead."

One night in 1975, for example, six months after he had won back his title, he was asked to appear at the award ceremony of a neighborhood Miami junior high school athletic conference. Even those who asked him were a little shocked when he accepted: There would be no money, no dinner, no publicity, not even a dais of local politicians to pat his head and promise to quash all his future speeding tickets. Just an auditorium of young athletes, white, black, and Hispanic, their families and girl friends, and a table of inexpensive medals and trophies.

Not only was Ali there, but he took over the evening, turning it into a rare event for the young people by never allowing the focus of attention to shift from their achievements to his. He delivered a short, warm speech, then kept up a steady commentary as each athlete came up for his award.

"Three medals in a row, uh-huuuuh. You really that good? . . . Look at this cool cat, he walks like Wyatt Earp. . . ."

At the end of the evening he accepted a cheap plaque for his troubles as if it were the championship belt. The hosts were beside themselves with gratitude; the champion had come to the people, had given them a memorable evening, and had done it with graciousness and wit, and *for free.*

Outside again, in the car that would return him to his wife and children, Ali watched hundreds of youngsters wave and shout and caper in the streets. All that was required of Ali now was a friendly wave as he drove away. The perfect end to a perfect evening.

Not Ali. He spotted a very pretty woman in a flowered print dress, an older sister of one of the young athletes. He opened the door against the crush and somehow pulled her into the car. They whispered together for a few minutes, then he wrote down her phone number for a future date before letting her out again.

Driving back, one of the hosts whispered to me, "Does he do this all the time? I'm not a prude or anything, but this isn't exactly what we had in mind."

Of course not. If there has been any pattern at all to Ali's life, any strand of consistency, it is this—he is never exactly what anyone had in mind.

The boxing businessmen who saw him, back in 1960, as a fresh, new drawing card never dreamed he would become the dominant financial figure in the sport and squeeze many of them out.

The civil rights activists who were delighted that he knocked Sonny Liston out of the spotlight never counted on Sonny's replacement being a segregationist.

The college students who applauded his antiwar stand were appalled by his antidope and antimixed dating stands.

Liberals who made him a symbol of the individual battling government oppression didn't expect him to be a sexist who clearly thought women should be subservient to men.

Black leaders who held him up as a symbol of black manhood must have winced as he mocked the southern accents and negroid features of other black boxers and called Joe Frazier a "gorilla."

International human-rights advocates may have been pleased when Ali offered himself as a link between the American black people and the "Third World." But they must have been uneasy every time he fought in an African or Asian country with a dictatorial regime he was thus supporting with his presence.

And his own Muslim coreligionists, with all their preaching about family respect, had to face the hypocrisy of a man who publicly chased other women while giving interviews on the responsibility of black husbands.

I don't have to be what you want me to be. I'm free to be who I want.

It's important to remember that Ali would never have even been in a position to fight for his rights if millions of brave men and women, black and white, had not fought for theirs through the history of the country. Ali owed particular debts to Jack Johnson, Paul Robeson, and Jackie Robinson.

Johnson was the first great black heavyweight champion of the twentieth century. While the original professional boxers in America were black slaves who sometimes won their freedom in the ring, the sport became predominately white in the nineteenth century: The blacks were squeezed out of boxing (as they had been squeezed out of horse racing and rowing) when money and prestige attracted whites.

Jack Johnson's incredible talent and flamboyance demanded attention. Once he won the title, a search began for "The Great White Hope" to beat him and assure white Americans they were really superior to the people they were oppressing. Johnson was viciously hounded from the ring and from the country. Ali's story contains echoes of Johnson's.

Paul Robeson was an all-America football player at Rutgers (and a Phi Beta Kappa) before he became a lawyer and then one of America's leading singers and actors. His courageous championship of human rights in a time of repression in the United States not only damaged his career but gave the elders of SportsWorld an opportunity to scratch his name off the all-America team—retroactively.

And Robinson, the first black in major-league baseball, a highly educated former Army officer, had to suppress his natural instincts as an outspoken, assertive, socially and politically involved individual so white America would "accept" him on the ballfield.

Without such real heroes, Ali could never have existed. And the cycle continues: Arthur Ashe, Reggie Jackson, Kareem Abdul-Jabbar, and thousands to come owe their increasing freedom as individuals, as blacks, as athletic figures, to Johnson, Robeson, Robinson . . . and Ali.

Late in 1975, in the Philippines, Ali again defeated his old rival, Frazier, in a brutal slugging match advertised as "The Thrilla in Manila." But he couldn't persuade Khalilah that just because he was heavyweight champion he had the right to leave her at home with their four children while he traveled with a tall, willowy California model named Veronica Porche. Within two years, Veronica was the third Mrs. Ali and the mother of two daughters, the champion's fifth and sixth children.

Ali's escalating financial responsibilities were often cited as the reason he continued fighting, but Angelo Dundee disagreed. "The key is, the kid likes boxing. He likes the sport, running in the morning, hanging around the gym, all the excitement building up to a title fight. And wouldn't you like something if you were the best in the world at it?"

But there was no doubt that Ali, by 1977, was in decline, that the powerful legs were no longer so limber—"I just can't dance all night no more," he admitted, "but who is the man he used to be?"—and he often seemed sluggish in the ring. Several times after lackluster performances he announced his retirement, but another big deal brought him back. Ken Norton for the third time, Alfredo Evangelista of Spain, Earnie Shavers, all fighters he would have toyed with in his prime, now gave him trouble. Ali at thirty-five was bored, according to his ring doctor of fifteen years, Ferdie Pacheco of Miami.

"Ali is now at the dangerous mental point," said Dr. Pacheco, "where his heart and mind are no longer in it. It's just a payday. It's almost as if an actor had played his role too long. He's just mouthing the words."

114

The fight doctor's ominous diagnosis was proven true on the night of February 15, 1978, a few weeks after Ali's thirty-sixth birthday. Leon Spinks, shorter, lighter, but twelve years younger, won a split decision in Las Vegas to replace Ali as the new heavyweight champion of the world.

It was a stunning upset, and a reminder of how Ali himself had originally won the title. No one gave Spinks a chance against Ali, just as no one had given Cassius Clay a chance against Sonny Liston fourteen years earlier. The experts dismissed Spinks—after all, he had fought only seven professional bouts (Clay had twenty before he fought Liston) and his only real claim to fame (just like young Cassius Clay's) was the Olympic gold *light*-heavyweight medal.

Ali didn't take Spinks seriously either. He did not train hard for the fight. He looked pudgy around the waist. And he was totally unprepared for young Spinks to stand and punch with him for fifteen grueling rounds, many more rounds than Spinks had ever fought before in one night.

Watching the fight, I remembered once asking Ali, back in 1965, if there was anyone who could beat him. And Ali replied, "The man who's gonna whup me is now ten years old. There's a little-bitty boy somewhere, walking around the sidewalk and he doesn't even know yet he's gonna get interested in boxing."

Leon Spinks, that little-bitty boy, was not intimidated by the legend of Muhammad Ali, a man who was a champion before Leon laced on his first boxing gloves. Spinks saw only the reality of Ali, a fading athlete already partially beaten by time.

When it was over, Ali looked bewildered and tearful. He said he would not retire, that he would now try to become the very first heavyweight in history to win the title for a *third* time.

Some people believed that a new goal would give him the energy and incentive to try harder. Others felt he should quit before he hurt himself and "tainted" his glorious story.

But if Ali was not a fighter, if he was not champion of the world, what could he do that would let him press hundred-dollar bills into the pockets of blind beggars or write a check for $100,000 to save a New York home for the handicapped Jewish elderly? One night he saw a newscast reporting that the home would have to close for lack of money, and the next morning he knocked on the door with the money in his hand.

"I couldn't believe it," he said later. "These poor crippled people came to this place to eat and talk with each other and draw a little and color, and that kept them alive. And no one else came up with the money. Didn't matter they were white or Jewish. Somebody's got to make a stand. Ain't nobody helping nobody in this country. It's dog eat dog. The dollar, the dollar, that's all they worry about."

And yet sometimes that was all he worried about. He talked about his homes and his cars and the money he gave his brother Rahman ("Fifty thousand a year just for drivin' and jivin' ") and his astronomical payrolls for trainers, cooks, bodyguards, public relations aides, sparring partners, drivers, business and

116

"spiritual" assistants, and just plain hangers-on to carry his bags and laugh at his jokes and listen to him talk about his real-estate deals and his import-export schemes and his securities investments and all the dollars he was going to make on the Muhammad Ali doll and the Muhammad Ali Saturday-morning cartoon shows and the Muhammad Ali bedsheets and the Muhammad Ali vs. Superman comic book and the Muhammad Ali movie and book and underarm deodorant.

But for all his money talk, his tastes were simple. He did not wear expensive personal jewelry nor did he even dress very well—for all but the most formal occasions, scuffed shoes, wrinkled slacks, and an open shirt were good enough. He might try to eat carefully while in training, but between fights a greasy fast-food-stand hamburger would do.

If there was any one thing he seemed to need beyond air and water and food, it was people around him. A few days before one fight, a friend and adviser, Harold Conrad, persuaded him to leave the midtown Manhattan hotel where people were calling him and banging on his door at all hours, and sleep at Conrad's uptown apartment. Ali became restless at the quiet and when Conrad tried to protect him from the occasional neighbor seeking an autograph, Ali would shout from the bedroom, "Send that old lady in, I want to talk to her."

One night, when Conrad and his wife had appointments, Ali asked, "You gonna leave me here all alone?" Apparently he had never been all alone before in his life.

It was inconceivable that he would ever willingly step out of the limelight, even after he finally quit boxing. He talked about becoming a diplomat, about running for office, about becoming a full-time minister of what was now called the World Community of Islam in the West. Elijah was dead and his son, Wallace Muhammad, had opened the group to white people and to the winds of change. Or Ali might become a television entertainer; he had made one successful television special, a variety show, and was always in demand as a guest.

His was the most recognizable face on the planet, and he wasn't going to hide it. What next?

When I ask him that question, sometimes he says he will become the world's greatest movie star and sometimes he says he will become the world's greatest businessman and sometimes he says he doesn't worry about such things, that Allah will tell him what to do when the time comes.

Once when I asked him that question he grew somber and stared at the ground.

"We're all like little ants," he said. "God sees all these little ants, millions of them, and he can't answer all their prayers and bless every one of them. But he sees one ant with a little influence that the other ants will follow. Then he might give that one ant some special powers.

"I'm like that special ant. Lots of other little ants know me, follow me. So God gives me some extra power."

We sat there, quietly, both thinking about this deep,

reverent, enormously self-important thing he had just said, until another reporter came by and joined us.

"What's up, Champ?" asked the other reporter brightly.

Ali looked up and winked. "Just hustling, ain't we all?"

Ali and You/
An Epilogue

Muhammad Ali once said, "I don't believe all the stuff I say."

INDEX

Taylor, General Maxwell D., 68–69
Terrell, Ernie, 68, 74, 77
Till, Emmett, 19–20
Time, 37
Tomorrow's Champions, 10–11, 13, 15, 19

U.S. Senate Foreign Relations Committee, 68
U.S. Supreme Court, 91, 98–99

Vietnam, 68, 71, 72–75, 91

Walcott, Jersey Joe, 59
Williams, Cleveland, 76
World Boxing Association, 74
World Community of Islam in the West, 118

Young, Andrew, 92